How a WAN Works.

Camboard Publishing
Cambridge. Great Britain.

www.camboard-publishing.com

Age range 11+

This book is designed for students who want to know the basics of how a wide area network works.

How a WAN Works explores the underlying concepts of how wide area networks function.

Combines full color illustrations that brings the inside of a network to life.

Describes the differences between local area networks (LAN) and wide area networks (WAN).

The network firewall is covered.

Describes data packets and ports.

The TCP/IP protocols are detailed.

Internet networks are covered.

Client Server is described.

Covers name server and peer to peer networks.

This full-color, fully illustrated guide to the world of wide area networks is ideal for computer science curriculums.

How a WAN Works.

Contents

Chapter 1

Introduction.

A network is a group of computers that are connected together.
The purpose of a network is to allow computers, to communicate with each other.

They are usually connected together by special cables.
Wi Fi can be used to allow cable free connections.

Networks

There are two types of networks that are commonly used.

A Local Area Network (LAN)

LANS are commonly found in:-

Offices
Factories
Schools
Hospitals

Local Area Network (LAN)

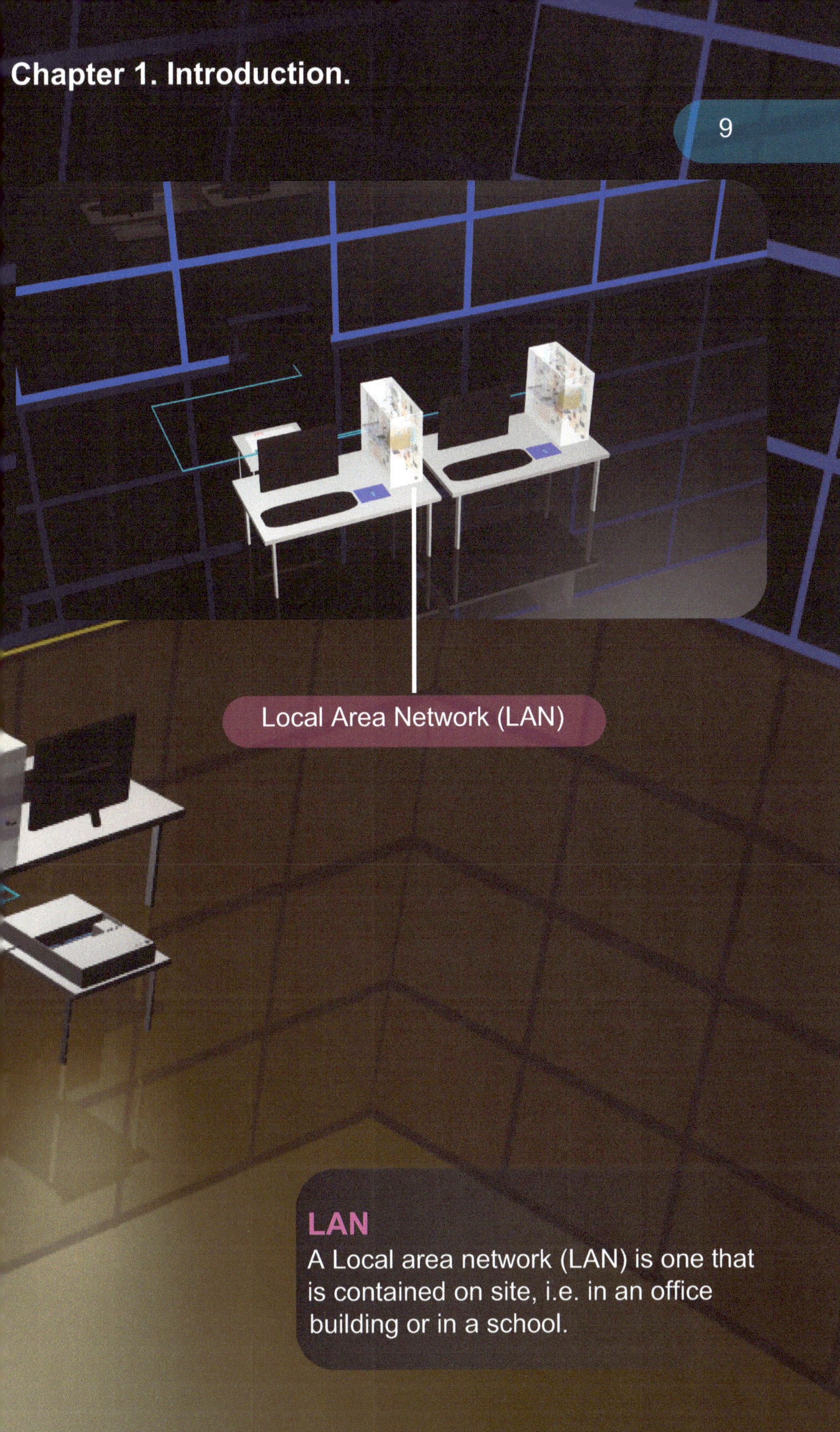
Local Area Network (LAN)

LAN
A Local area network (LAN) is one that
is contained on site, i.e. in an office
building or in a school.

WAN

A wide area network (WAN) is one, that is not situated in one building.

It can be computers in offices, that are situated throughout the world.

Internet

The internet is in effect a wide area network.

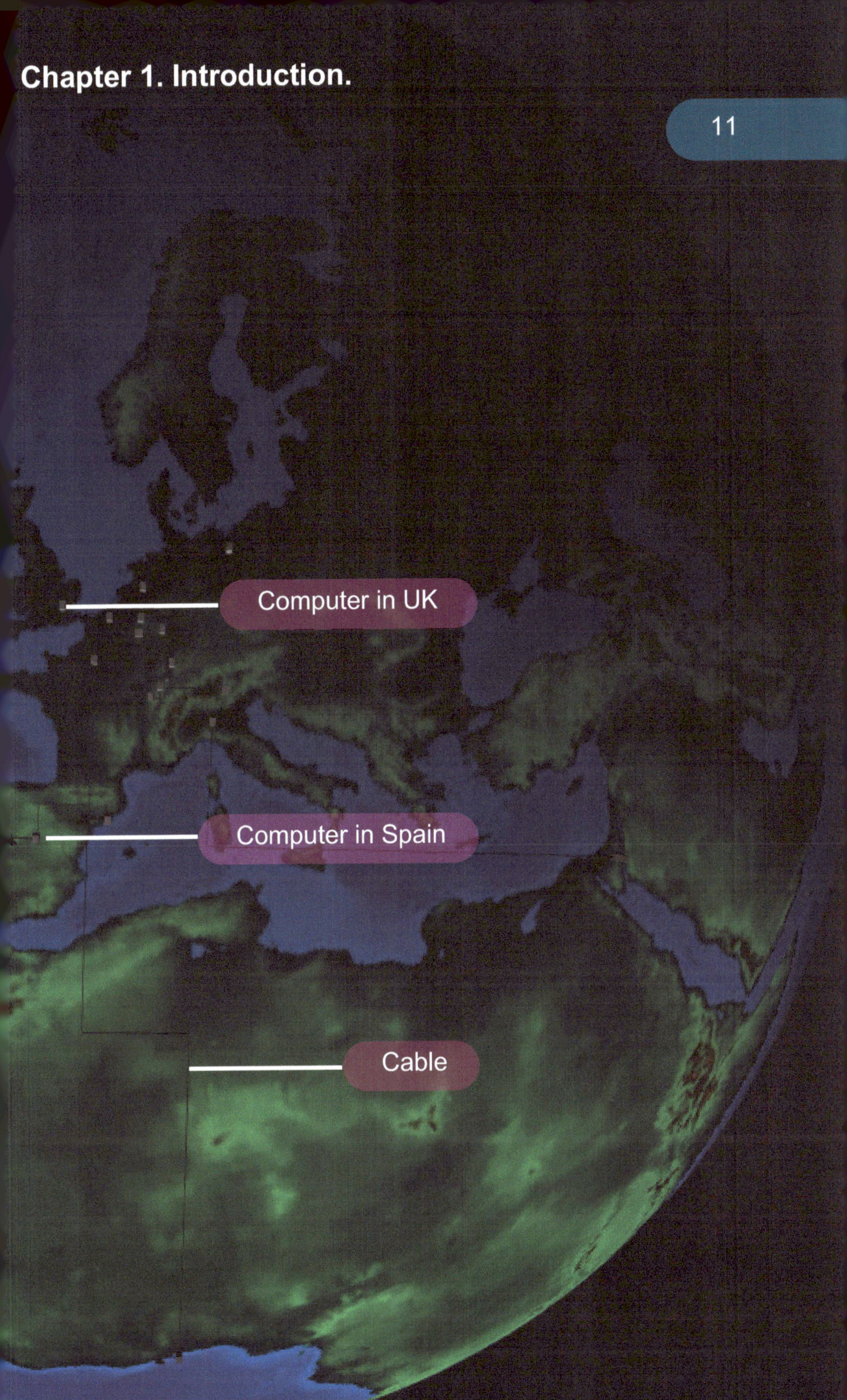
Computer in UK
Computer in Spain
Cable

Wide Area Network

A WAN (Wide area network) is a group of connected computers, that are not situated in one building.

The WAN is used by a company to connect computers in one office, together with another office in a different location.

LAN in Spain

Offices

Offices can be located anywhere in the world, it's quite common to find huge groups of local area networks in an office connected into a WAN.

LAN in German Office

Data.

The data transferred between locations, can be transferred over the internet.

With some large companies they use their own private networks, to carry data over continents to their overseas offices.

Fiber Optic Cable.

Data is transferred over long distances using fiber optic cable.
Fiber optic cable enables data to be transmitted at the speed of light.

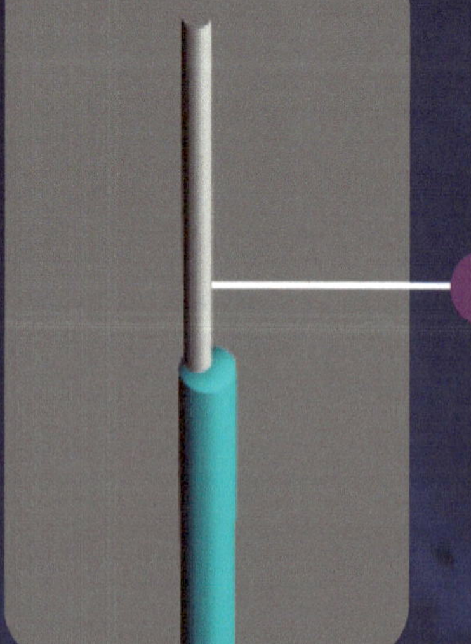

Chapter 1. Introduction.

Data moving through cables.

Fiber Optic Cables

Data can travel over land by fiber optic cable, or under the sea in huge arrays of fiber optic cables.

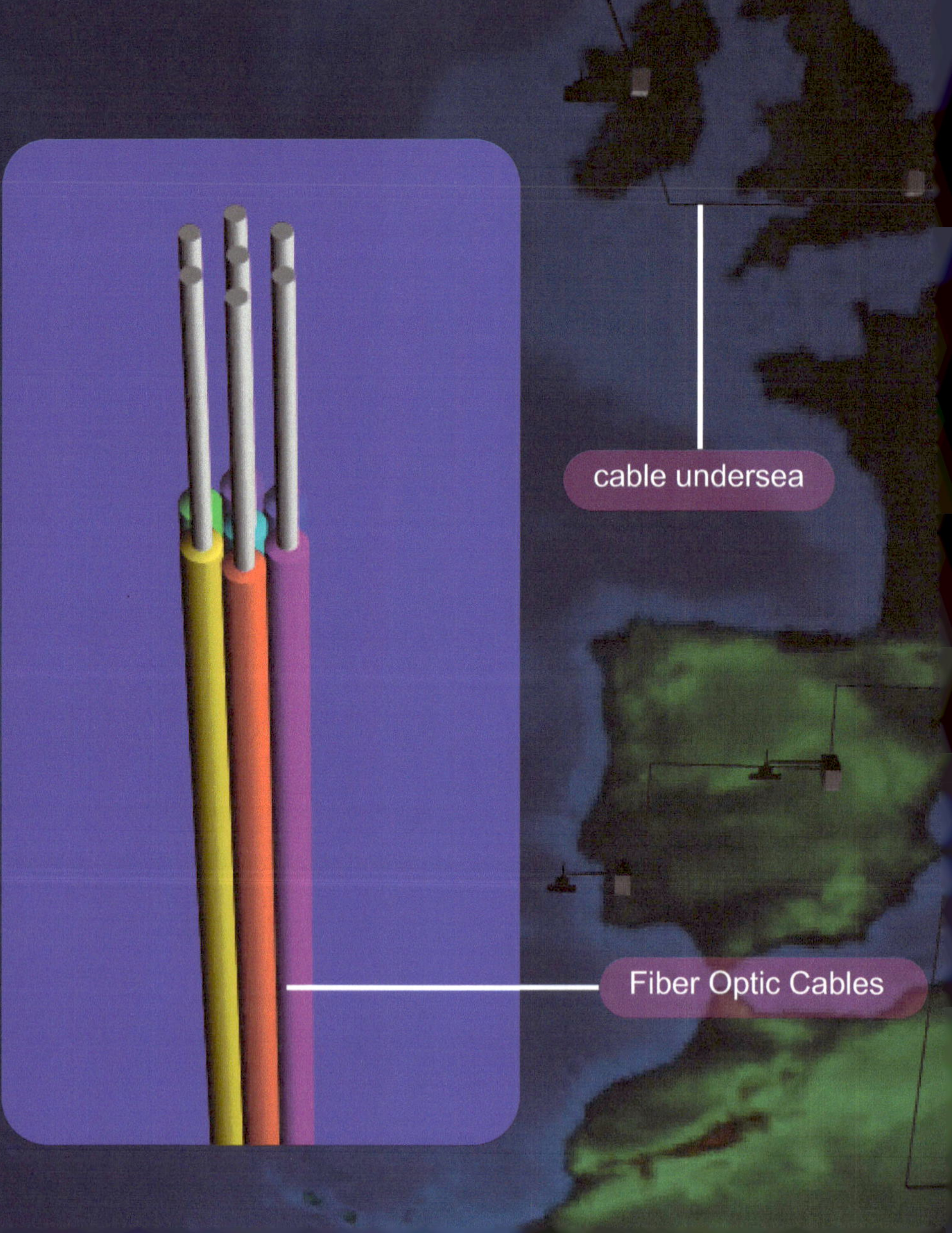

cable undersea

Satellites

Satellites are used for transmitting data to some remote locations.
Satellites are often used where there is no cable or mobile data transmission available.

Satellite Dish

A ground station with a large satellite dish, picks up the beam from the satellite in orbit.

The data is then fed into a cable network.

Satellite

Chapter 2

Client Server.

Clients

A client server network, refers to a network of computers called clients.

These clients connect to a computer called a web server.

This computer contains web pages that any of the client computers can access.

Web Servers.

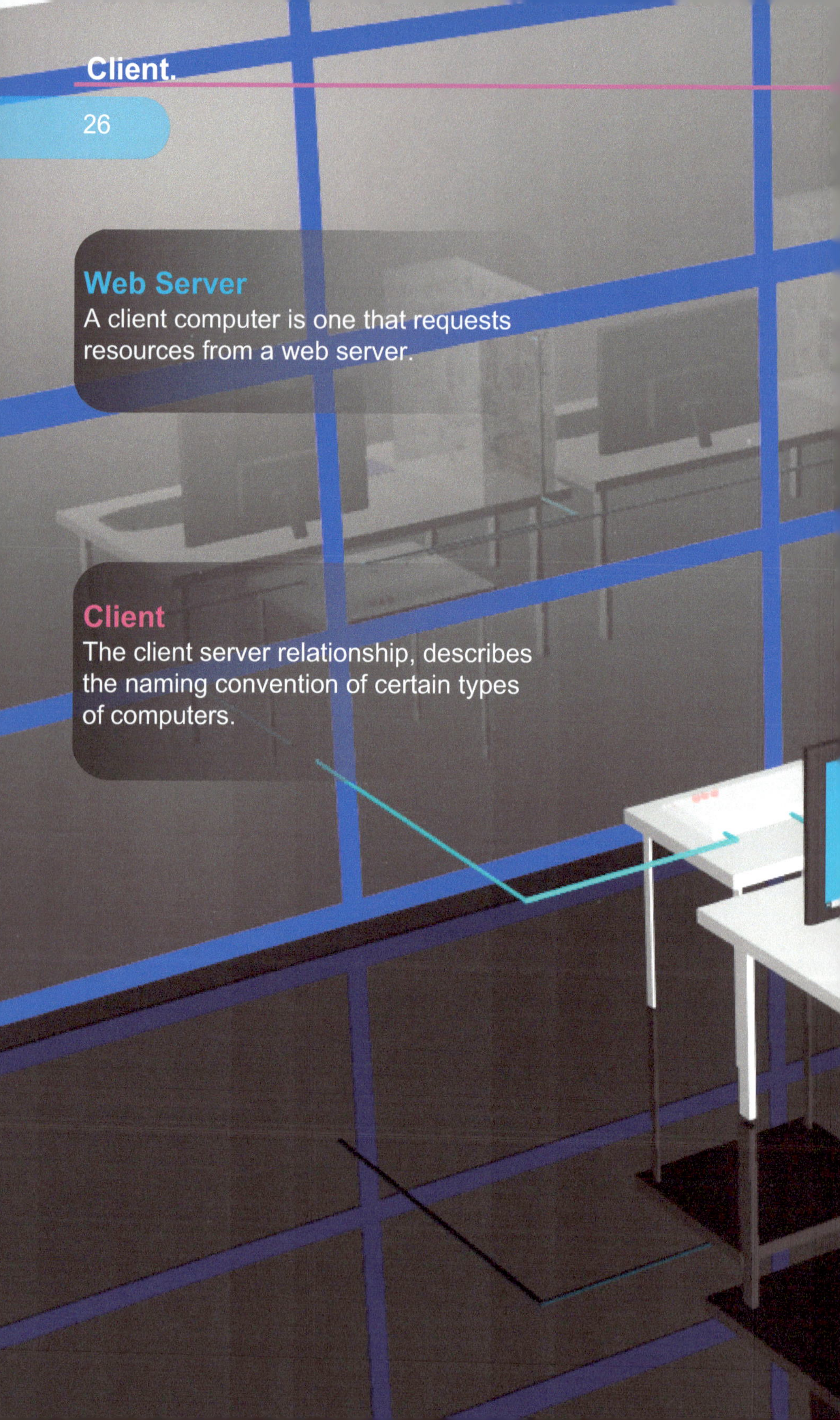

Web Server

A client computer is one that requests resources from a web server.

Client

The client server relationship, describes the naming convention of certain types of computers.

Chapter 2. Client Server.

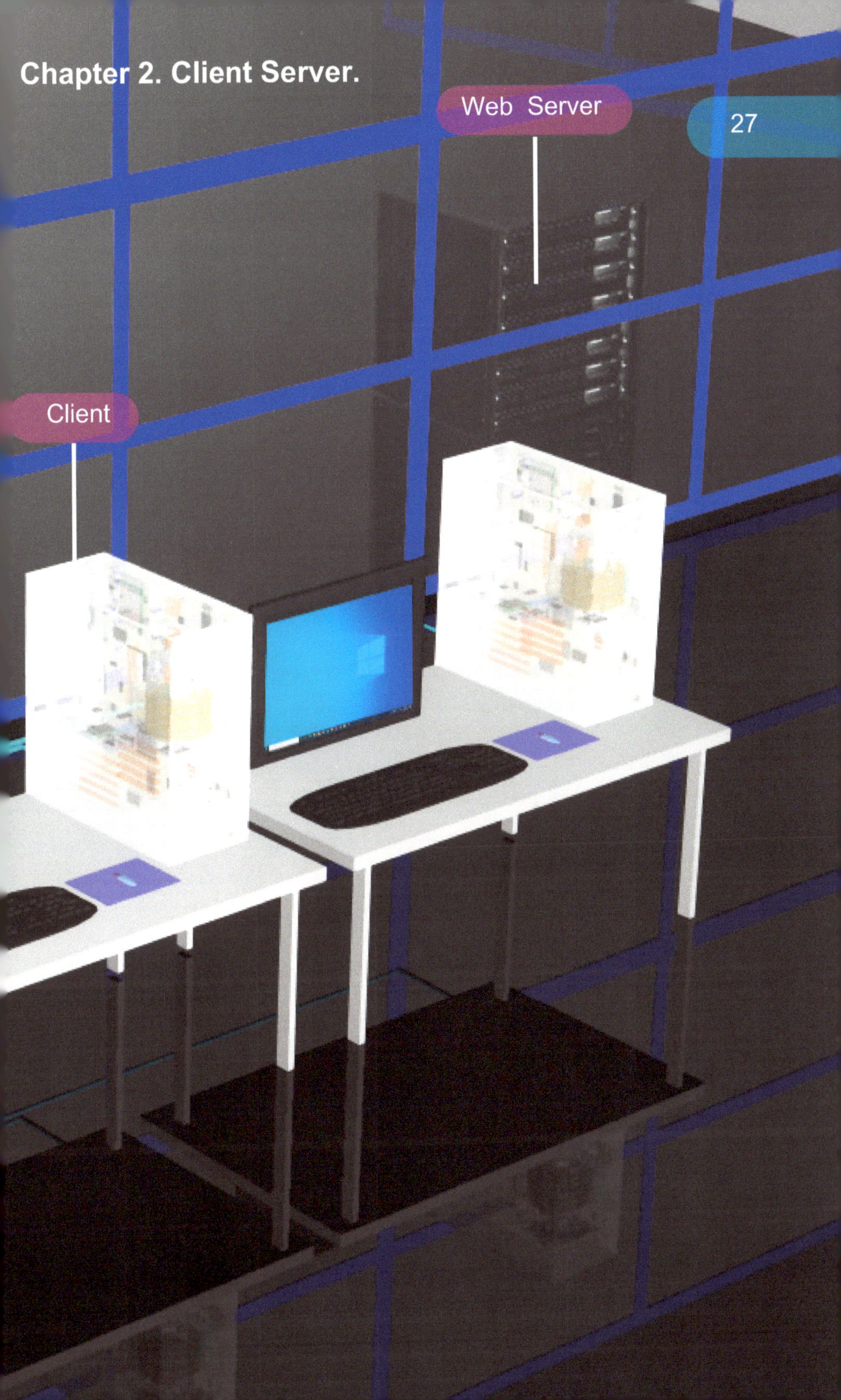

Client Computer

Web pages

Web pages are often requested by a client computer.

A web server stores the pages, and makes the page file available to the client computer on request.

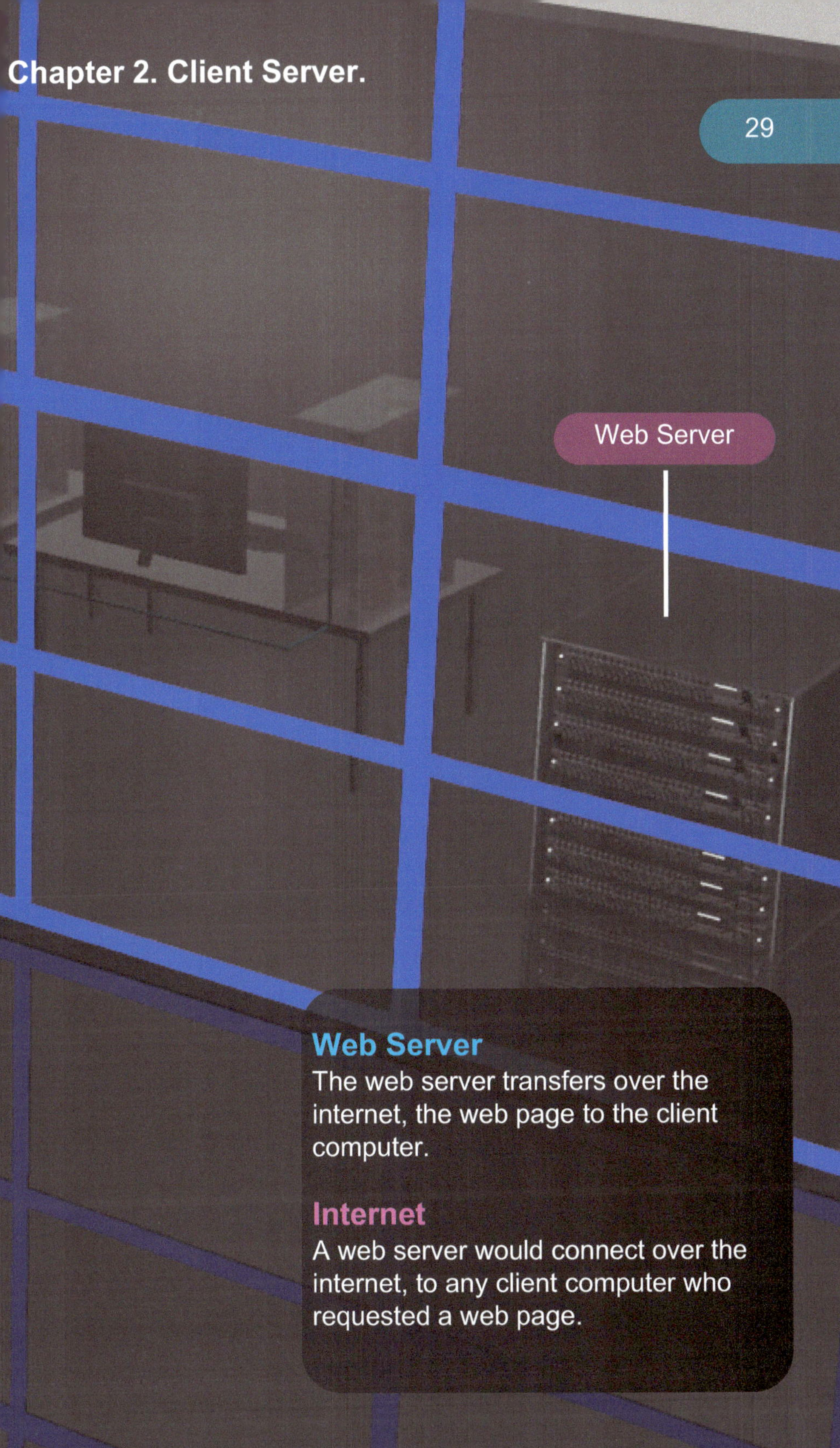

Web Server
The web server transfers over the internet, the web page to the client computer.

Internet
A web server would connect over the internet, to any client computer who requested a web page.

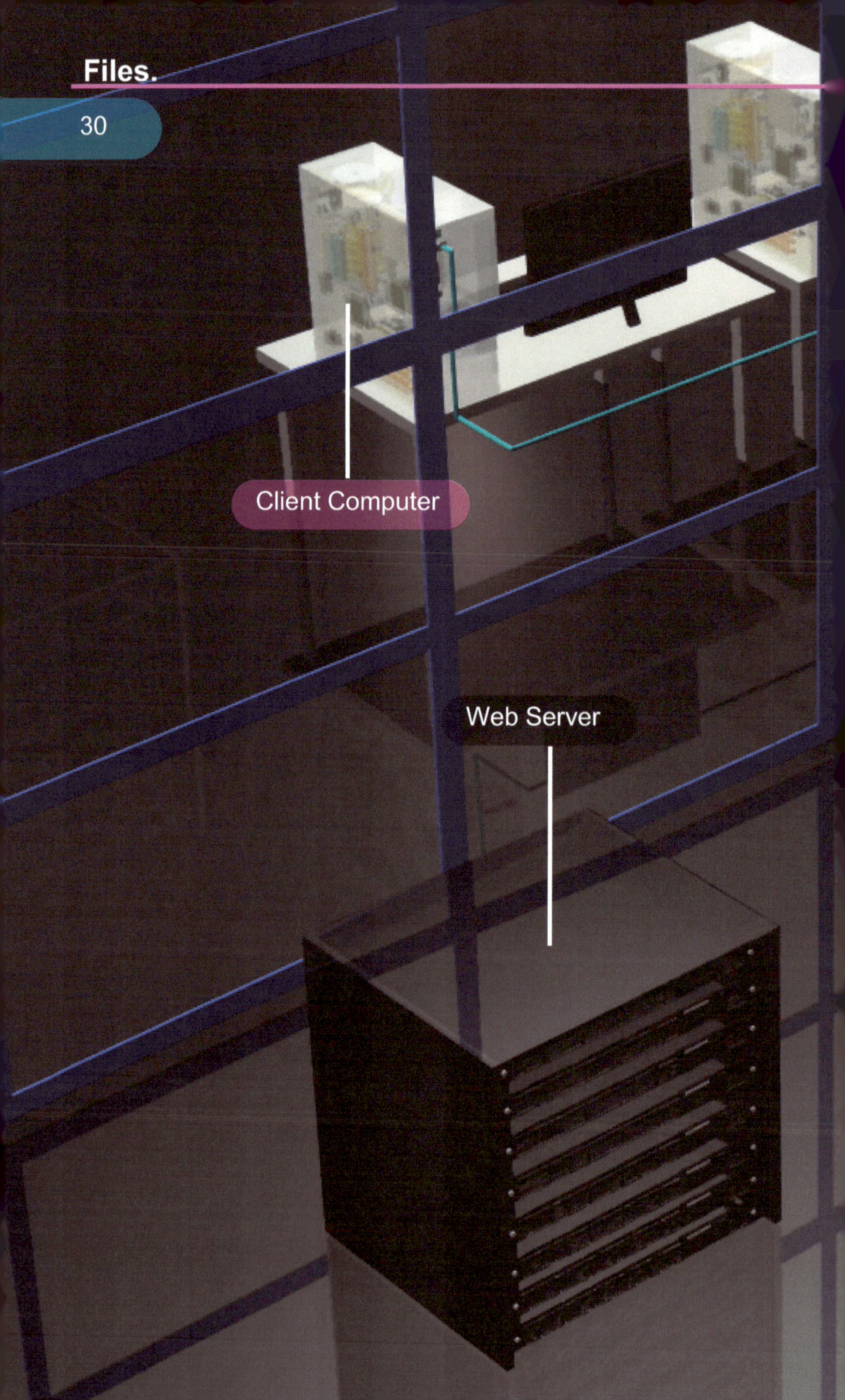
Client Computer
Web Server

Web Server
The web server connects to the internet, this enables any client computer on the internet to request a web page file from the server.

Network Switch
The web page travels through an ethernet cable to the network switch.

Internet
The web page travels through various routers, before it is transfered to the client computer that requested the web page.

Chapter 3

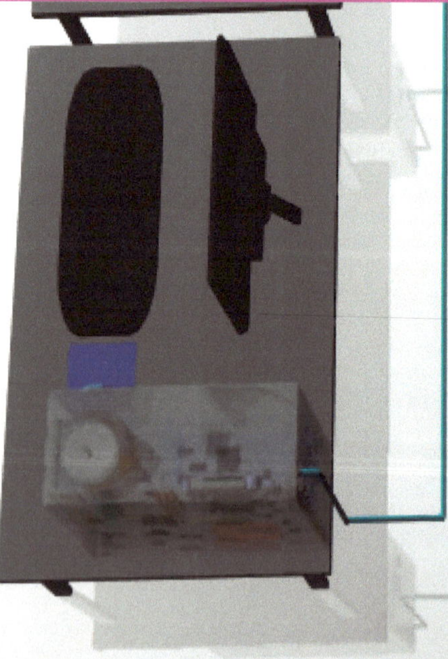

FireWall.

FireWall

Because we often don't know if someone is trying to gain access to our computer through the internet, we use a firewall to control who can access the computer and what data we will accept.

Local Area Network
A hardware based firewall that is based in the network switch, will physically stop blocked data getting into the Local area network computers..

The Firewall is a piece of software or hardware, that analyses data that comes into your network or computer.

This stops certain data that we don't want getting onto the network of computers.

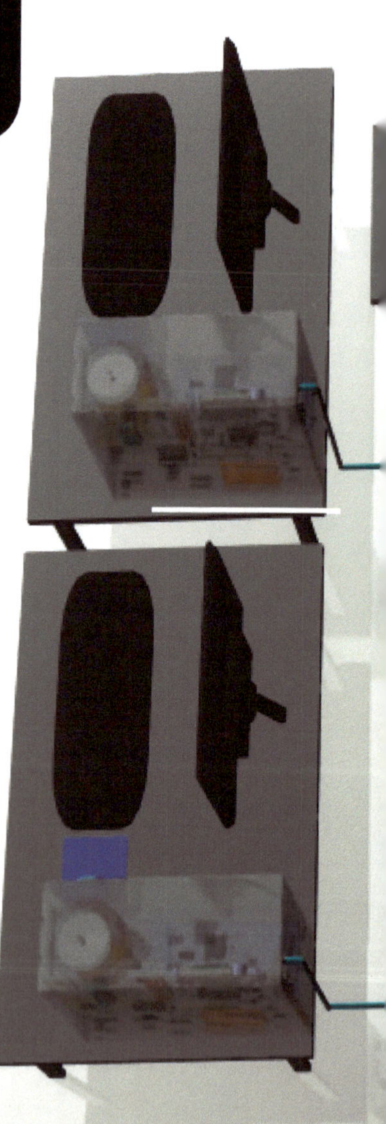

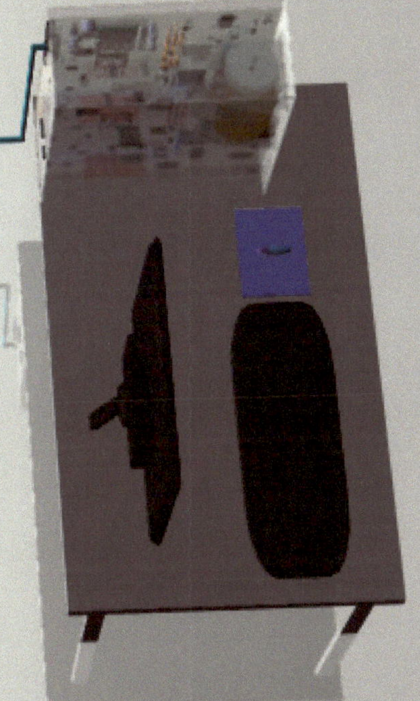

Network

A firewall is often incorporated into a network router.
This is because unwanted data can be rejected before it gets onto the network.

Data Packet
Each piece of data that comes into the
network is combined in a data packet.

Metadata
Each packet has metadata.
The metadata contains information such as
the destination IP address, and where the
data is from.

Network
The firewall reads this data and
decides whether to accept it onto the network.
If the data is accepted, its routed to the PC
that requested it, otherwise the data is
rejected.

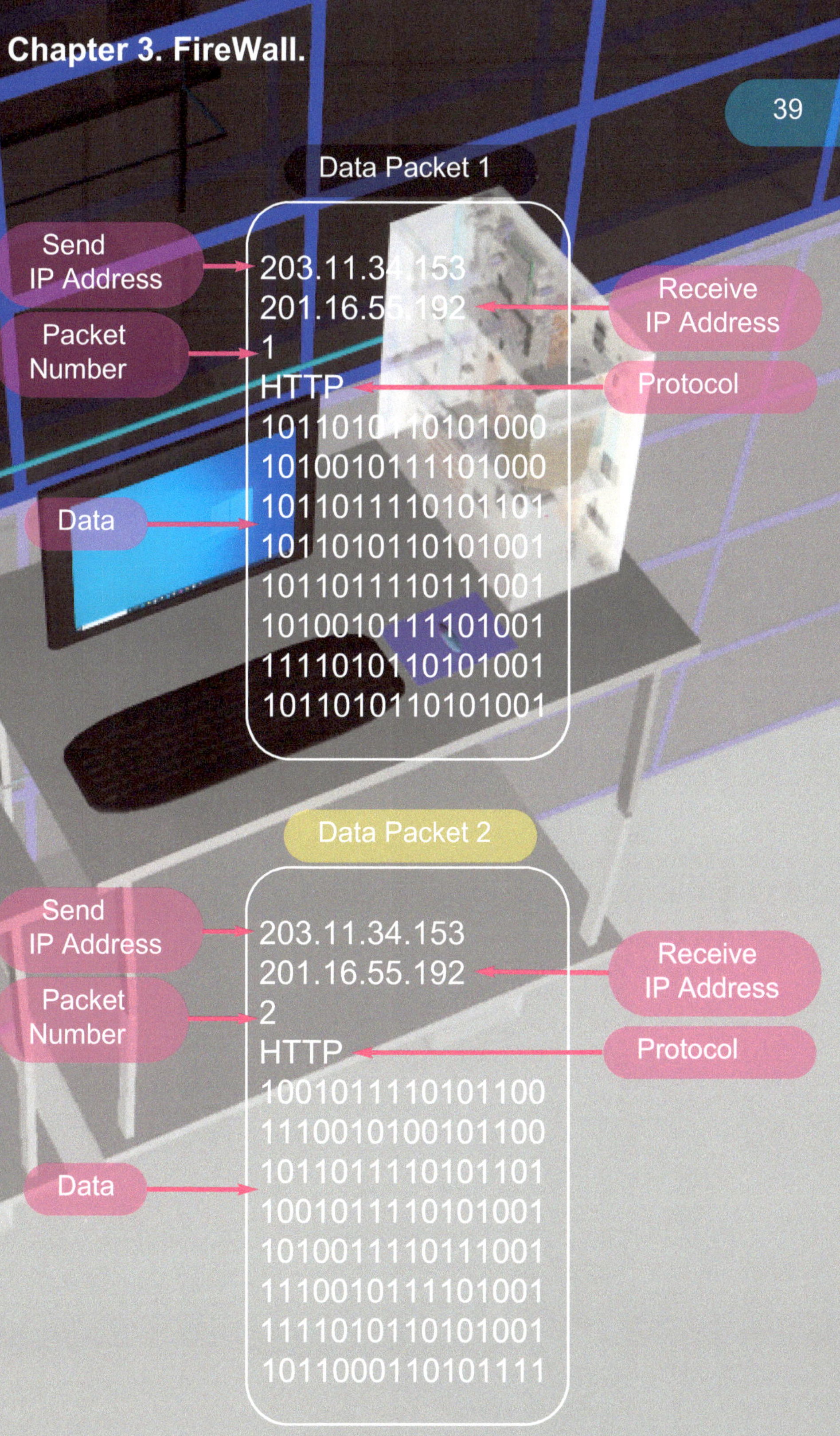
Data Packet 1
Send IP Address
203.11.34.153
201.16.55.192
Receive IP Address
Packet Number
1
HTTP
Protocol
10110101 10101000
10100101 11101000
10110111 10101101
10110101 10101001
10110111 10111001
10100101 11101001
11110101 10101001
10110101 10101001
Data
Data Packet 2
Send IP Address
203.11.34.153
201.16.55.192
Receive IP Address
Packet Number
2
HTTP
Protocol
10010111 10101100
11100101 00101100
10110111 10101101
10010111 10101001
10100111 10111001
11100101 11101001
11110101 10101001
10110001 10101111
Data

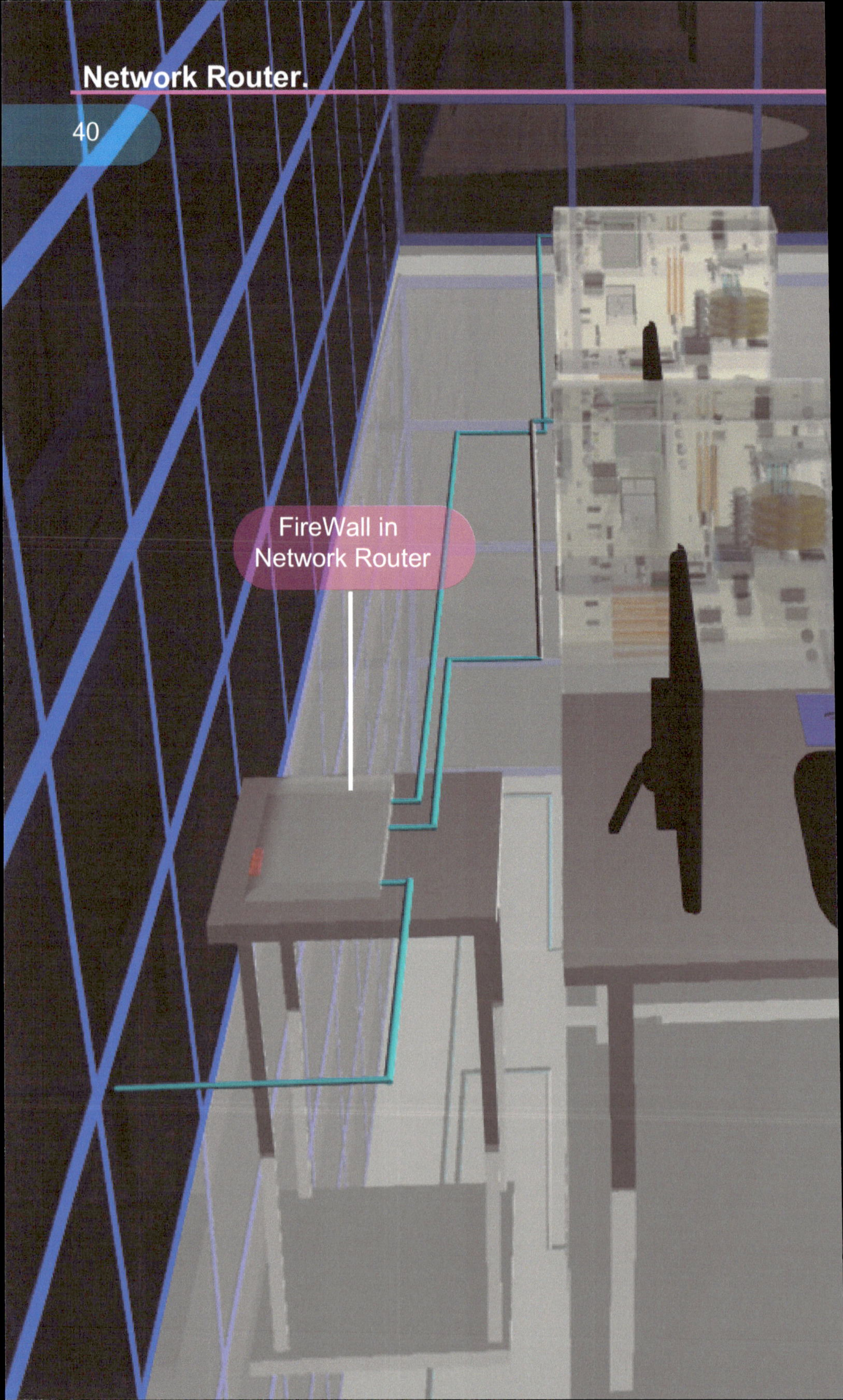

Network Router.
40
FireWall in
Network Router

FireWall

The firewall has a set of rules that govern what sort of data the firewall will let through or reject.
With Windows a firewall program is included, that lets you control access to ports.

Every computer has connection ports that accept certain types of data through.

HTTP is accepted through port 80.
FTP is accepted through ports 20-21.

You can close these ports to stop access to your computer.

This is done by changing the ports rules on your firewall software.
With windows a firewall program is included, that lets you control access to ports.

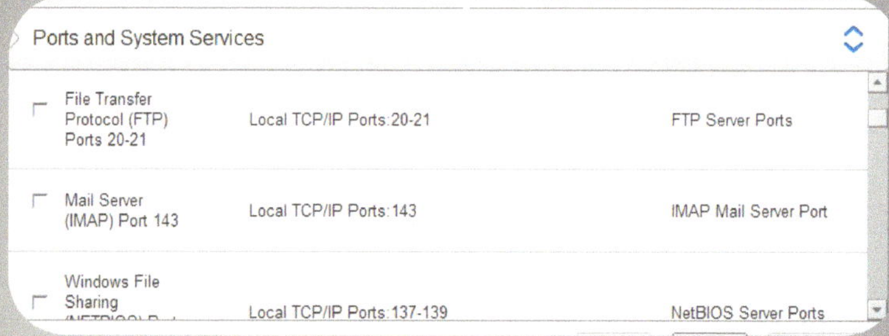

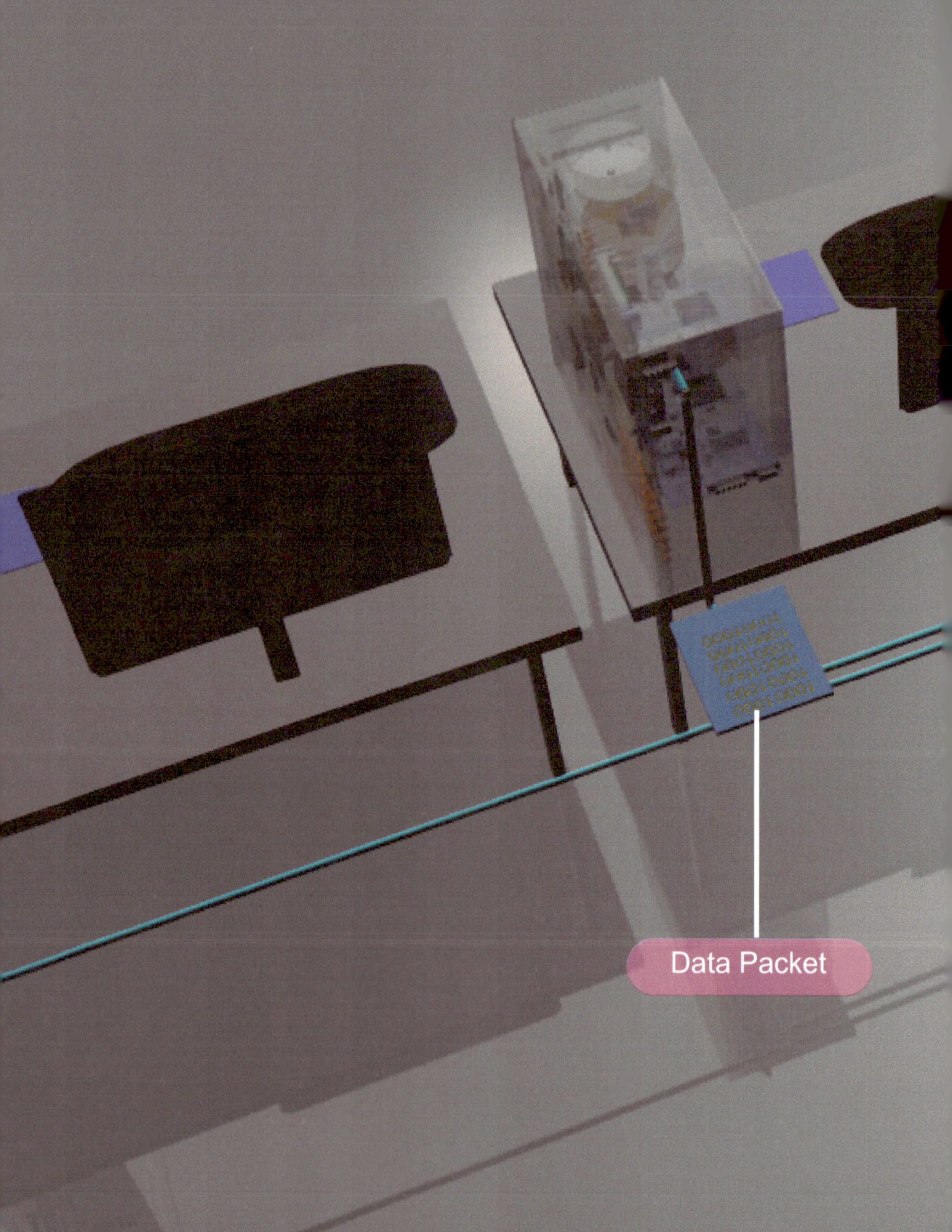
Data Packet

Data Packets
The firewall will analyse the data packets sent through any of the open ports, if for instance a data packet received on port 80 used the FTP protocol it would be rejected.

Firewall
Firewalls are important to stop unauthorized users gaining access to the files on your computer.

Chapter 4

Data Packets.

Internet

Data that travels through the internet to your network, is grouped together in a data packet.

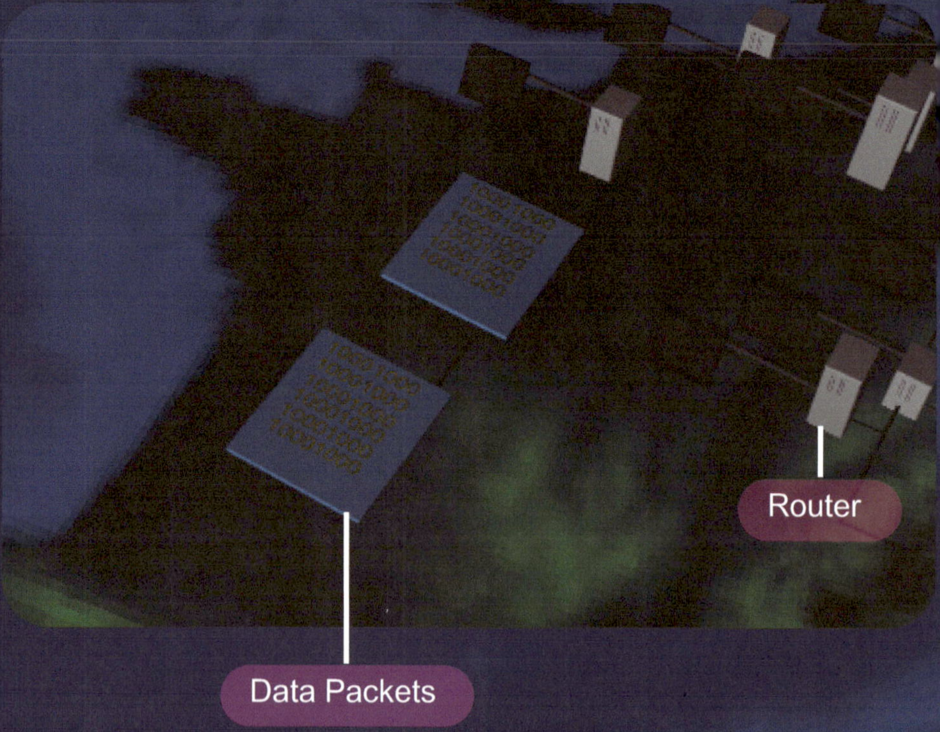

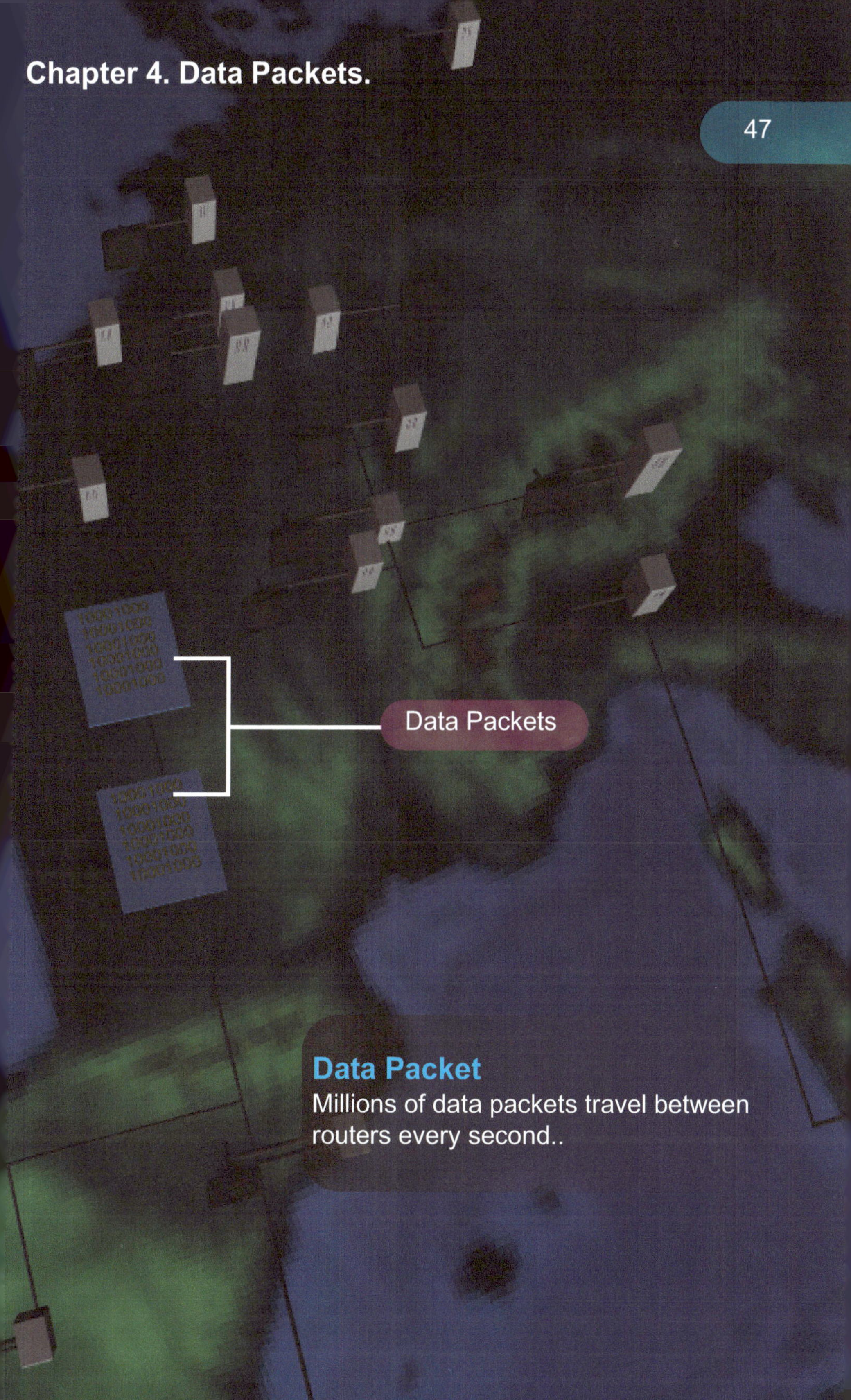

Data Packet

Millions of data packets travel between routers every second..

Packet Inspector

At the top of the packet is metadata.

This metadata tells the packet inspector software, where the data came from, this would be the senders IP address.

The recipients IP address is also included.

Send IP Address

Packet Number

Data

203.11.34.143
201.16.55.192
1
HTTP
1011010110101000
1010010111101000
1011011110101101
1011010110101001
1011011110111001
1010010111101001
1111010110101001
1011010110101001

Receive IP Address

Protocol

TCP

Data moving the Internet, uses TCP/IP protocols.

Transmission Control Protocol (TCP) is the transport layer responsible, for how the data is packetized.

The transport layer is responsible for the encapsulated data, contained in the data packet.

Popular transfer layer protocols are:-
HTTP (HyperText Transfer Protocol). Used for web pages.

FTP (File Transfer Protocol). Used for transferring files.

SMTP (Simple Mail Transfer Protocol). Used for Email.

These protocols use specific ports on your computer.
HTTP uses Port 80.
FTP uses Ports 20-21.

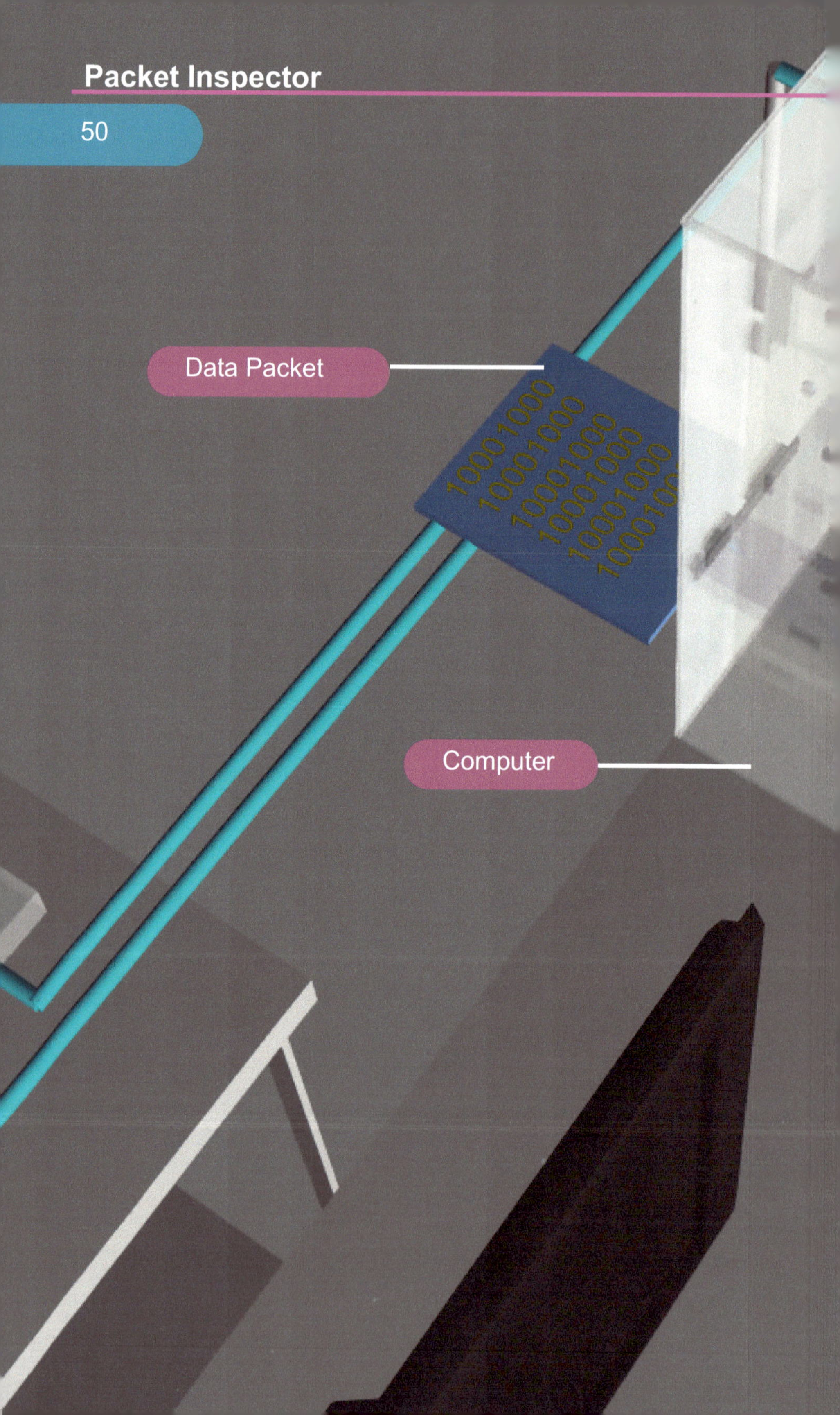

Packet Inspector
50
Data Packet
Computer
10001000
10001000
10001000
10001000
10001000
10001000
10001000

Packet Inspector

The packet inspector software determines whether the computers IP address, matches that in the data packet.

IP Address

If it does not the packet will be rejected. When the IP addresses match, a check is made of the senders IP address. If the senders IP address is on a block list, the data will be rejected.

Data Packet

Chapter 4. Data Packets.

Port

Once these tasks are satisfied the data itself will be checked, for which network protocol is used.
If the port is closed the data packet will be rejected.
When the port is open the data will be accepted.

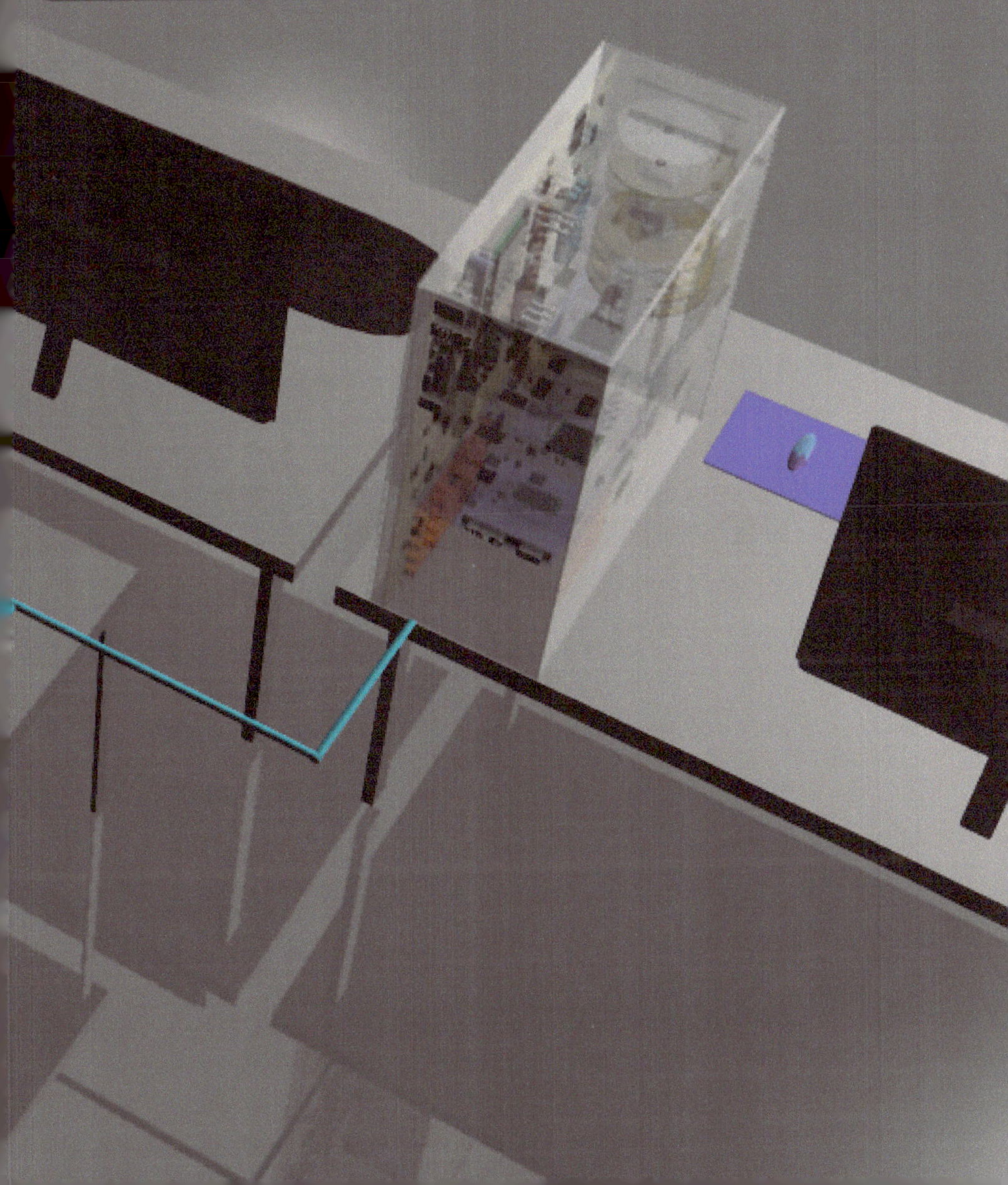

HTTP

The data packet is transferred to the program, that deals with data that is specified in the protocol.

The HTTP protocol would route data to a web browser.

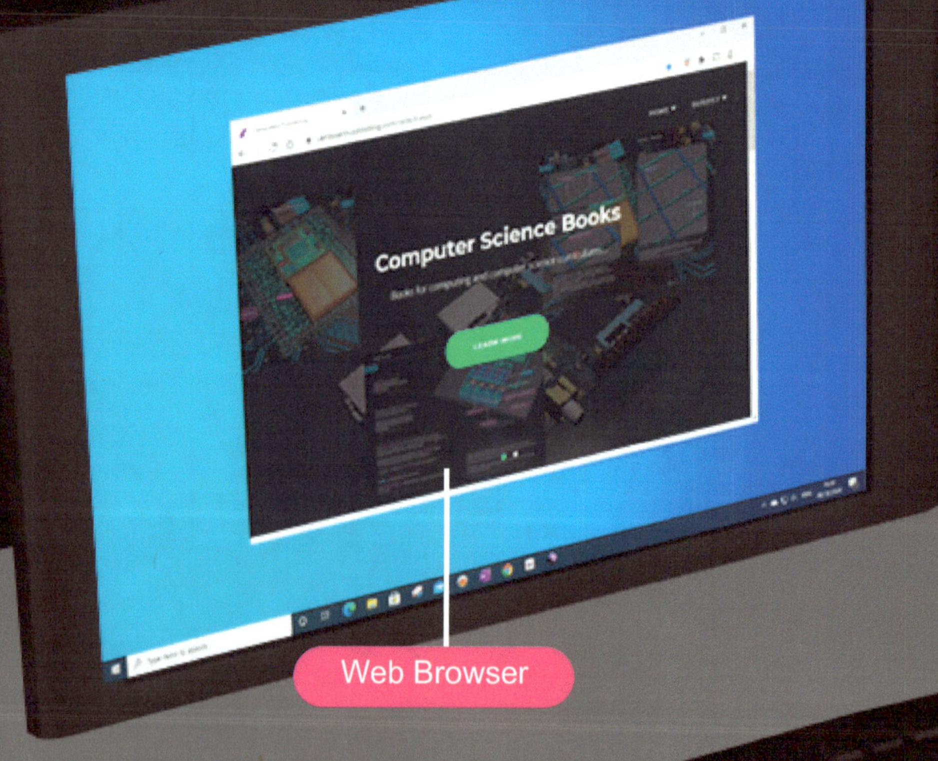

Web Browser

File

Once all the data packets are received,
they are joined up to make one file.
This file is read by the computer.

Chapter 5

Protocols.

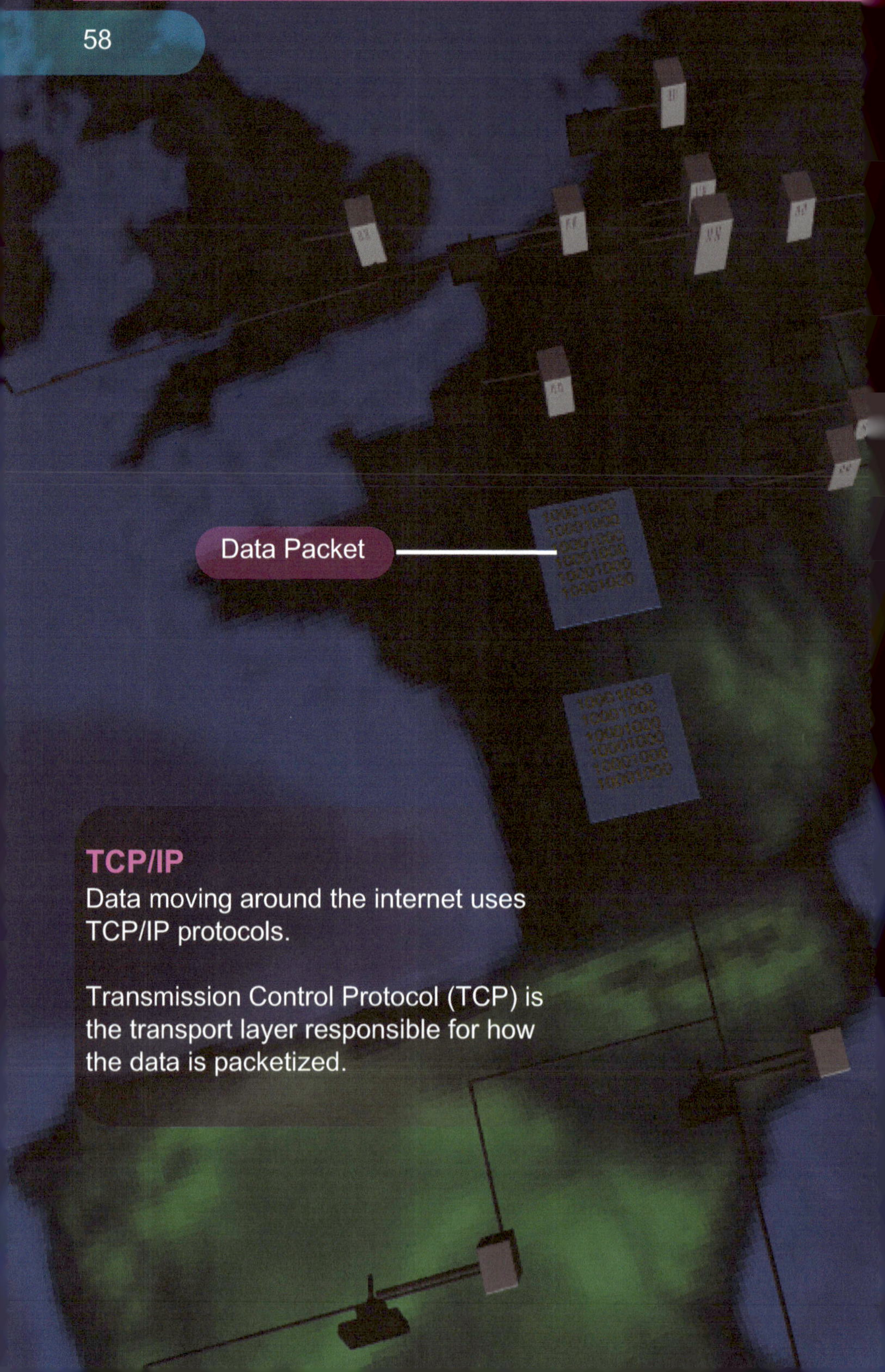

Data Packet.

TCP/IP

Data moving around the internet uses
TCP/IP protocols.

Transmission Control Protocol (TCP) is
the transport layer responsible for how
the data is packetized.

Data Packet

The TCP standard is responsible for
how the data packet is organized.
It sets out the order of what data is in
the header packet.

Header Packet

The header packet is what comes
before the actual data.

This would be:-
Senders IP Address
Receive IP Address
Packet Number
Protocol

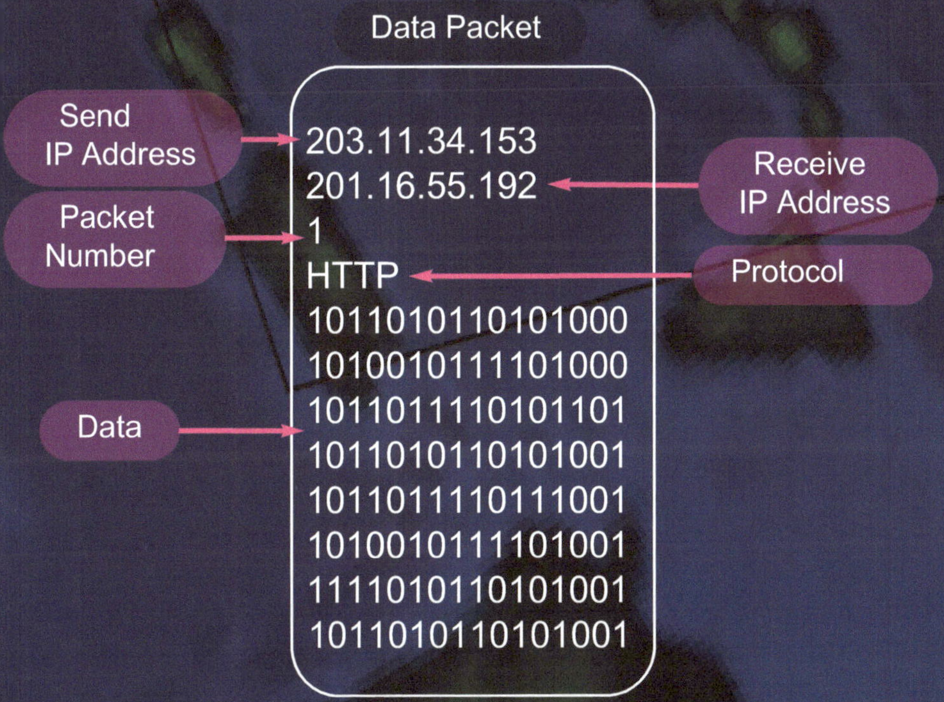

Data Packet

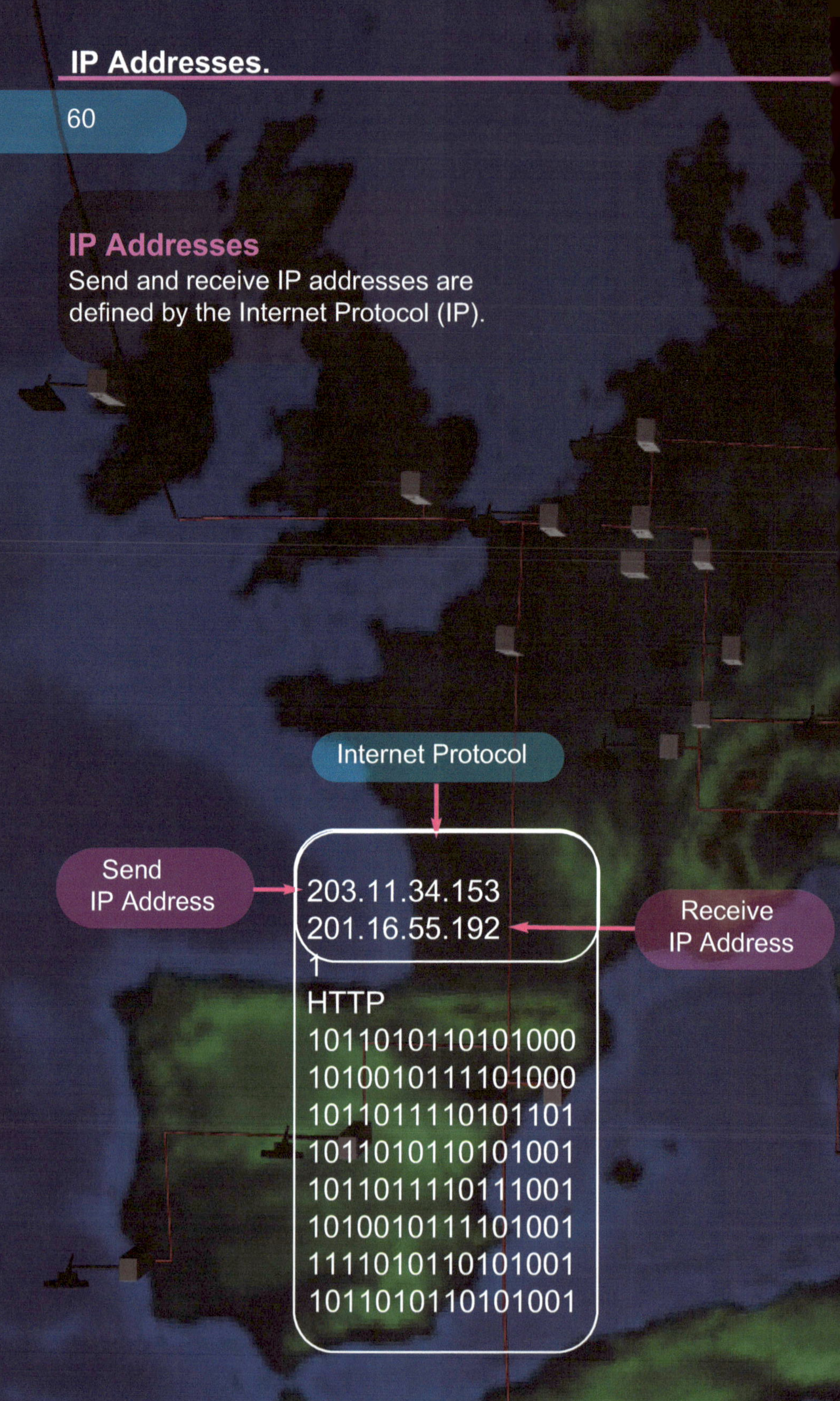
IP Addresses.
60
IP Addresses
Send and receive IP addresses are
defined by the Internet Protocol (IP).
Internet Protocol
Send
IP Address
203.11.34.153
201.16.55.192
Receive
IP Address
HTTP
1011010110101000
1010010111101000
1011011110101101
1011010110101001
1011011110111001
1010010111101001
1111010110101001
1011010110101001

Internet Protocol

Internet Protocol (IP) is the internet layer responsible, for routing the data through various routers in the internet.

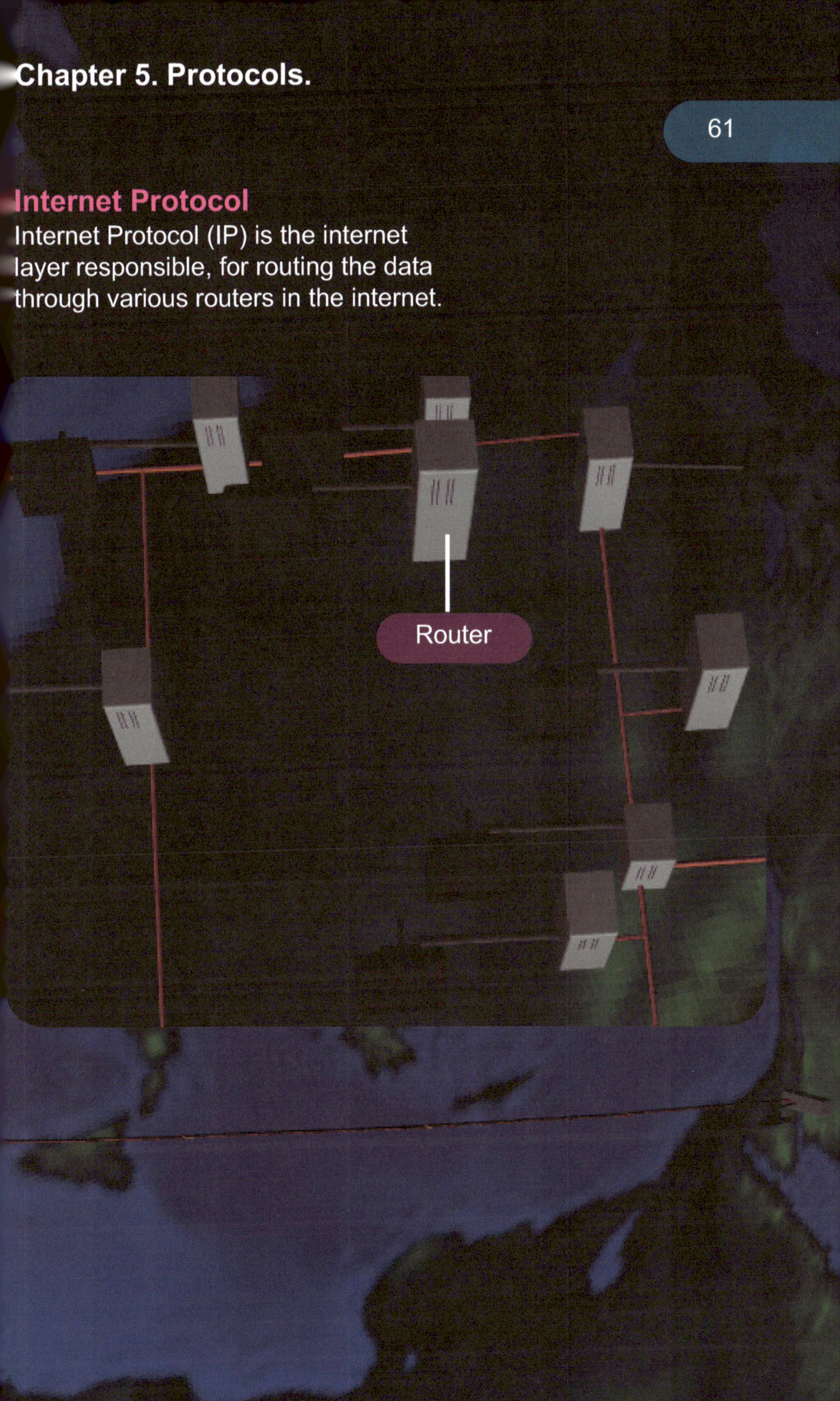

Transport Layer

The transport layer is responsible, for the encapsulated data contained in the data packet.

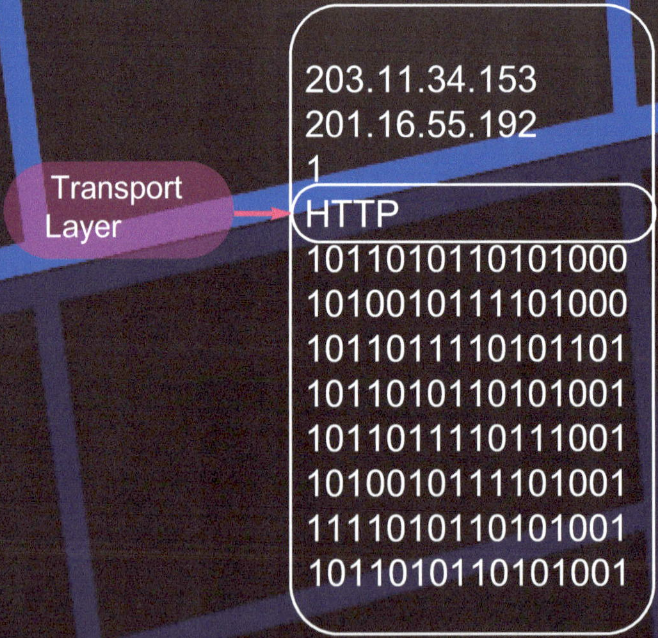

Transport Layer

203.11.34.153
201.16.55.192
1

HTTP

1011010110101000
1010010111101000
1011011110101101
1011010110101001
1011011110111001
1010010111101001
1111010110101001
1011010110101001

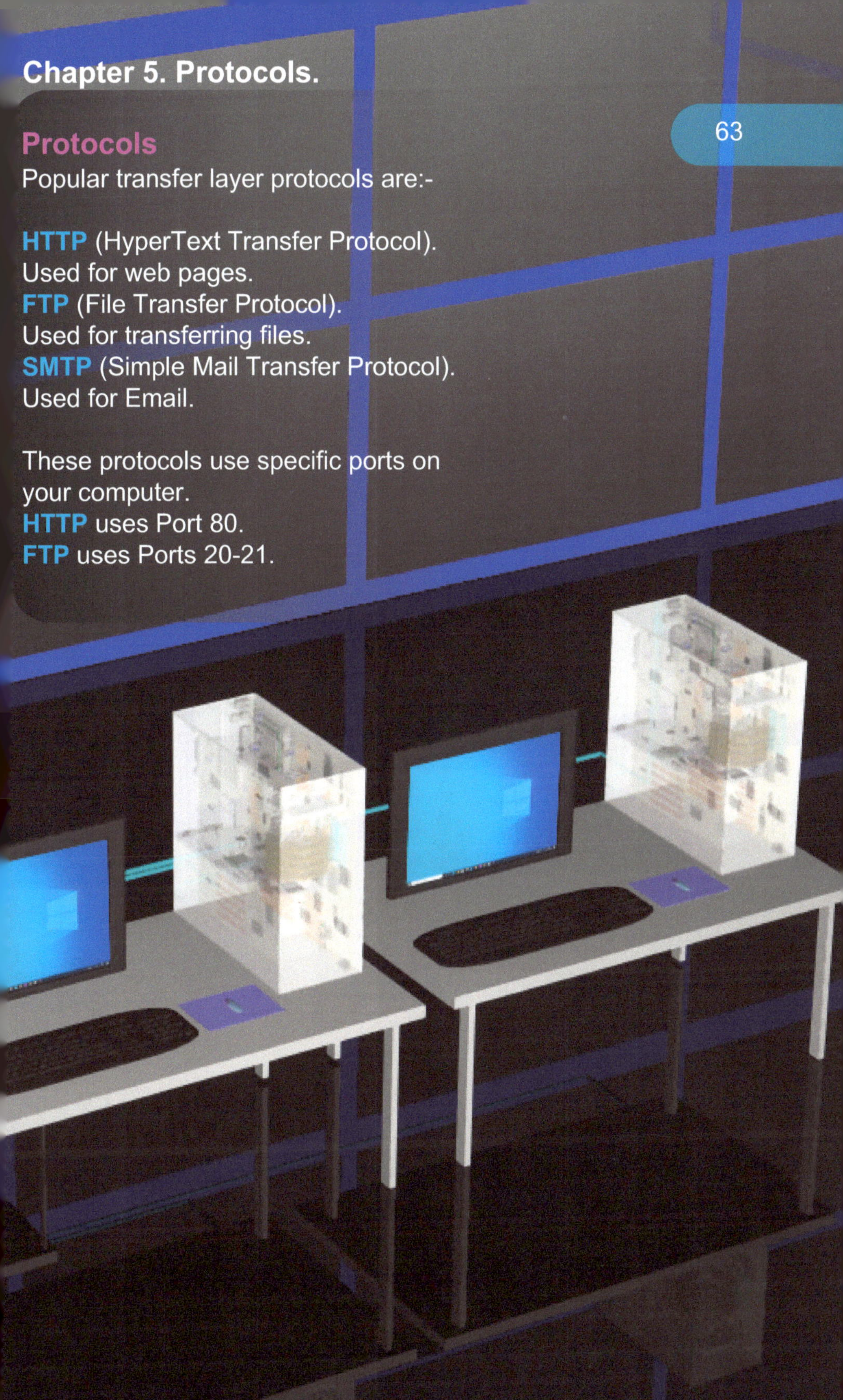

Chapter 5. Protocols.

Protocols

Popular transfer layer protocols are:-

HTTP (HyperText Transfer Protocol).
Used for web pages.
FTP (File Transfer Protocol).
Used for transferring files.
SMTP (Simple Mail Transfer Protocol).
Used for Email.

These protocols use specific ports on
your computer.
HTTP uses Port 80.
FTP uses Ports 20-21.

Chapter 6

Internet.

Internet

The internet is a huge connected
network of computers.
Millions of computers across the world,
are connected together to form the
biggest network in the world.

Undersea Cable

Fiber Optic Cable

Data moves through fiber optic cable
underground. Huge data capacity fiber
optic cables, are laid at the bottom of
the sea to connect continents together.

Satellites

Satellites connect countries on one side
of the world, to a country on another
side of the world.

Satellite

Data Centers

Data centers across the world contain huge numbers of servers, that host millions of web pages, handle millions of emails each day.

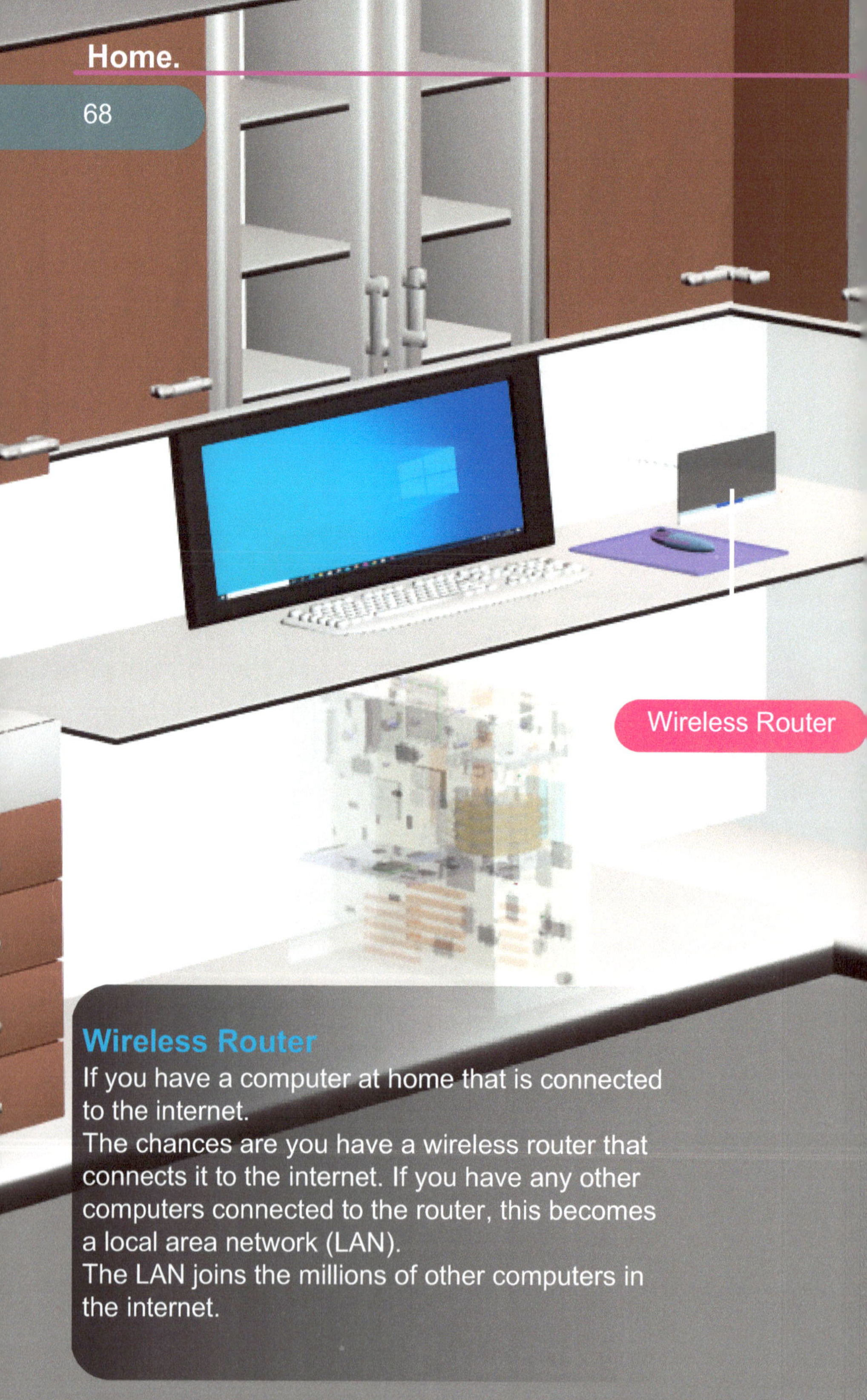

Wireless Router

If you have a computer at home that is connected
to the internet.
The chances are you have a wireless router that
connects it to the internet. If you have any other
computers connected to the router, this becomes
a local area network (LAN).
The LAN joins the millions of other computers in
the internet.

Wide Area Network (WAN)

When you switch on and connect to the internet, your computer joins the millions of other computers in the internet.

Your computer then becomes part of the wide area network (WAN).

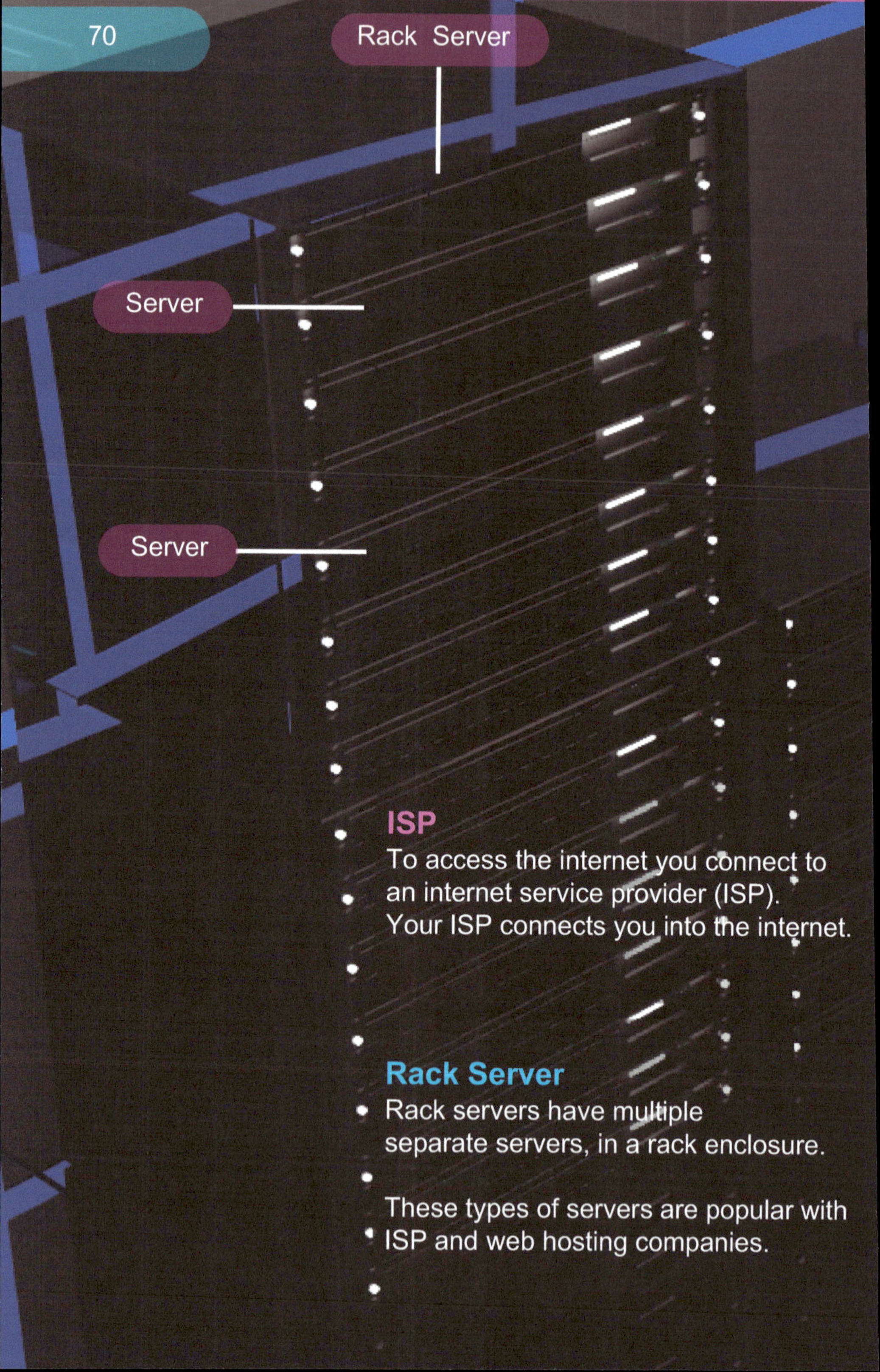

ISP

To access the internet you connect to an internet service provider (ISP). Your ISP connects you into the internet.

Rack Server

Rack servers have multiple separate servers, in a rack enclosure.

These types of servers are popular with ISP and web hosting companies.

Domain Name Server

Router

Servers

Your ISP will have a huge number of servers.
These servers will have different purposes.
Some servers will have modems in, these will connect to your wireless router.

DNS

When you request a web page from a site, the ISP will look up the address of the site on its Domain Name Server (DNS).

Web Page

When it finds the address for the web page, another server called a router will connect to another router in another building, probably in a different country. The router will then access a web server, with the web page on and retrieve the page.

Internet Services

Once your' connected you can access
different internet services like:

World Wide Web (WWW)
Electronic Mail (Email)
Chat and Instant Messaging
Internet telephony

Chapter 6. Internet.

Data Packets
All these services use packets of data
that travel through the Internet.

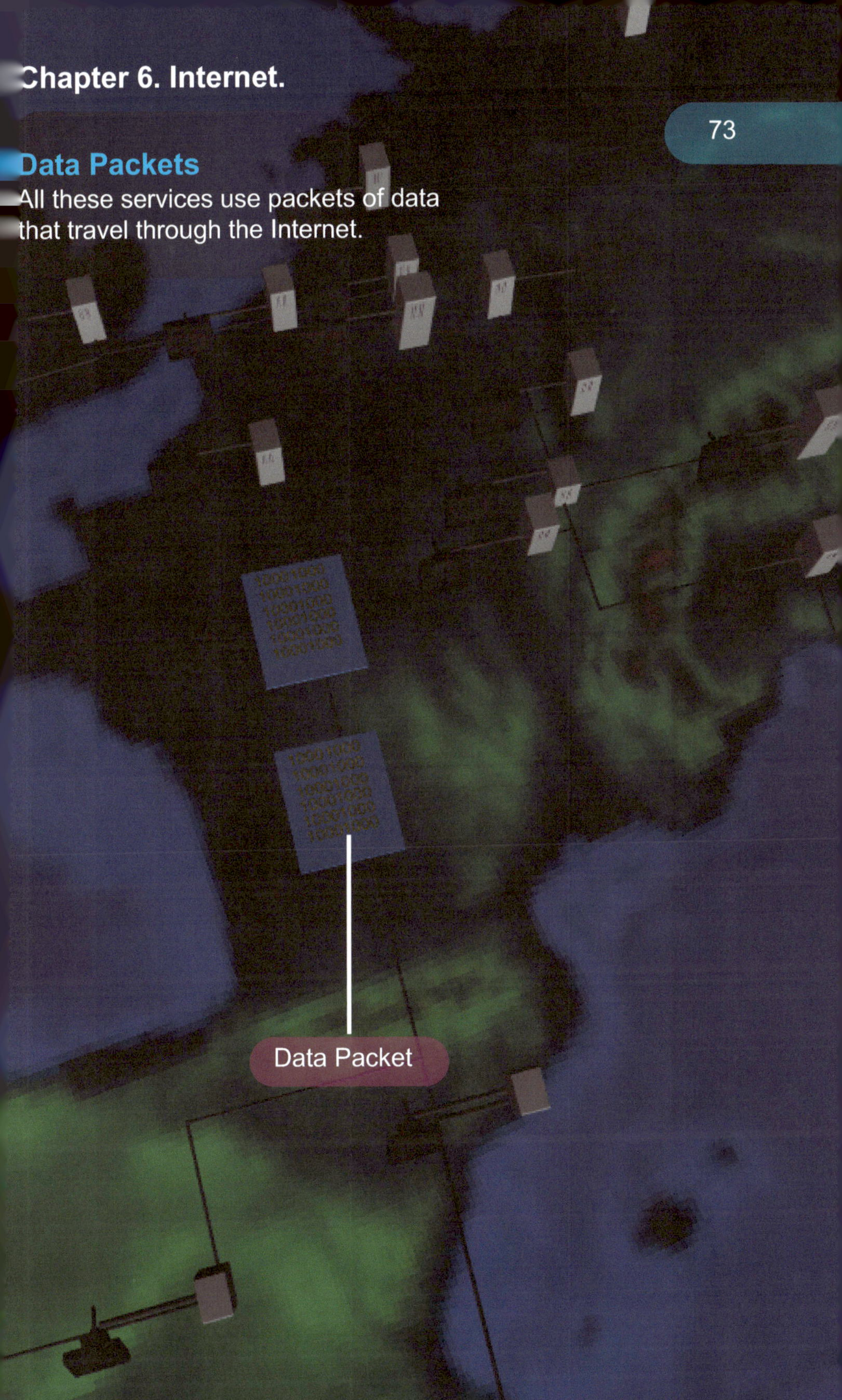

Data

The internet contains a huge network of servers, that contain vast amounts of data.

Server

A server connects to routers, that enable your computer to find them on the internet.

Cable

Huge amounts of cable, connect all of these computers together.

Chapter 6. Internet.

Satellites

The internet also uses satellites to transmit data.

Satellites transmit data between themselves in orbit and then transmit data to a ground station.

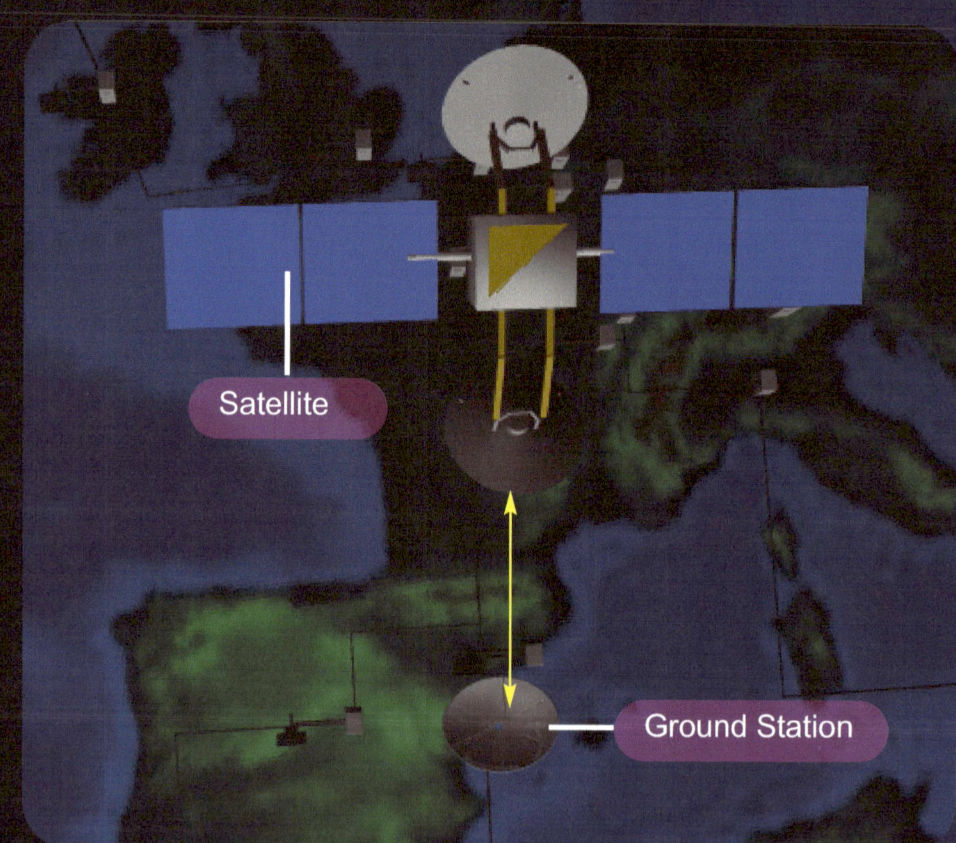

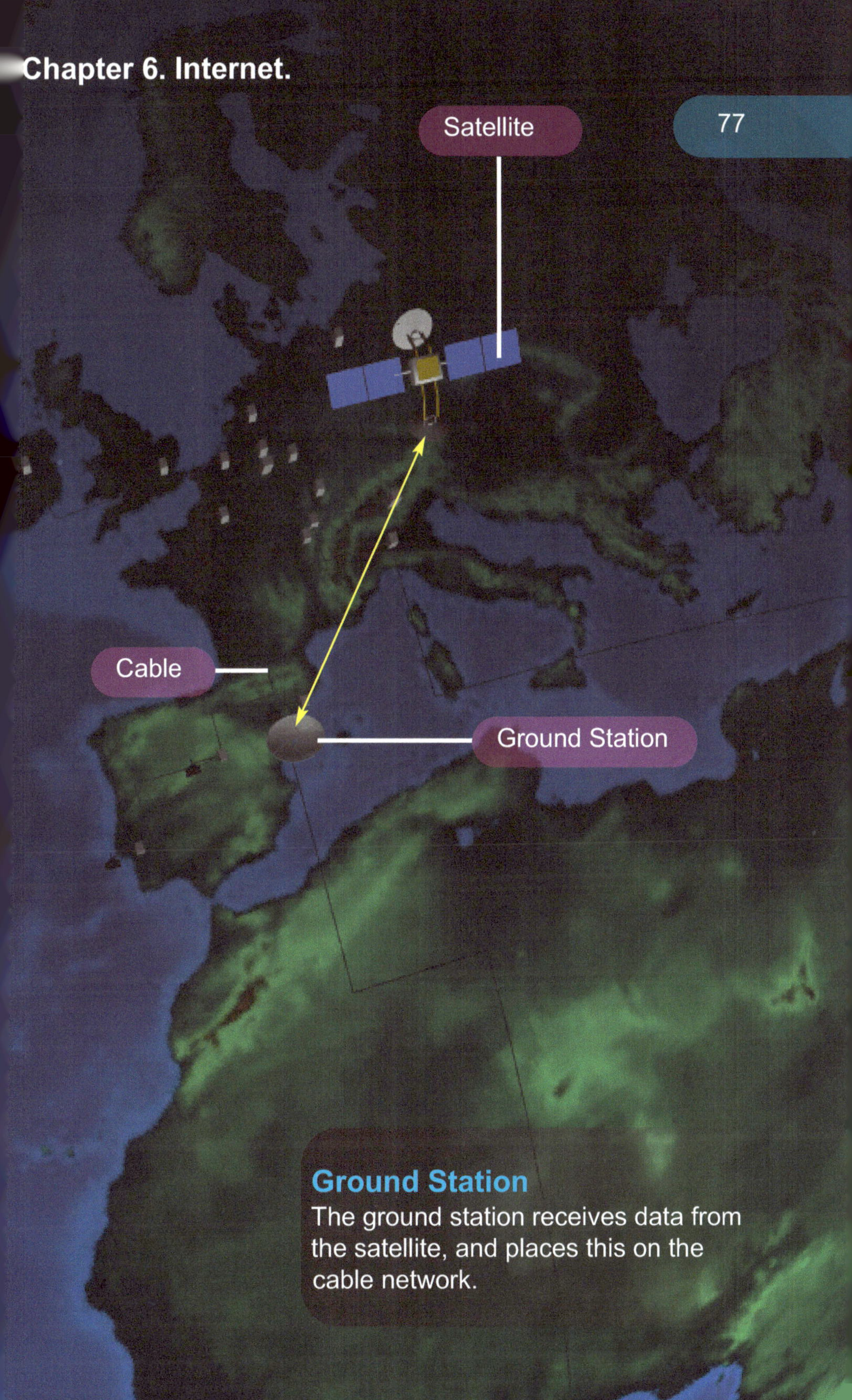

Ground Station

The ground station receives data from the satellite, and places this on the cable network.

Chapter 7

Name Servers.

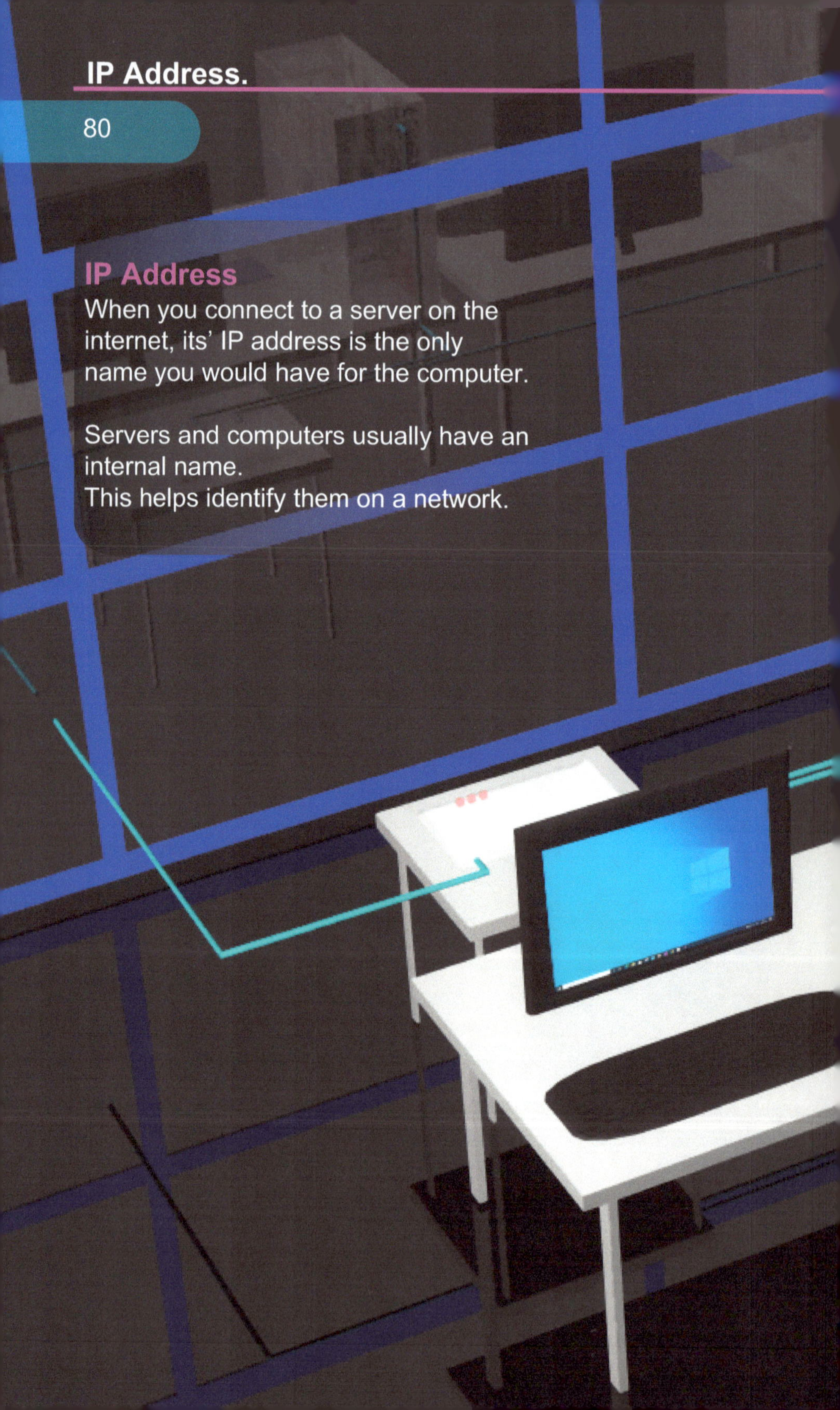

IP Address.

IP Address

When you connect to a server on the
internet, its' IP address is the only
name you would have for the computer.

Servers and computers usually have an
internal name.
This helps identify them on a network.

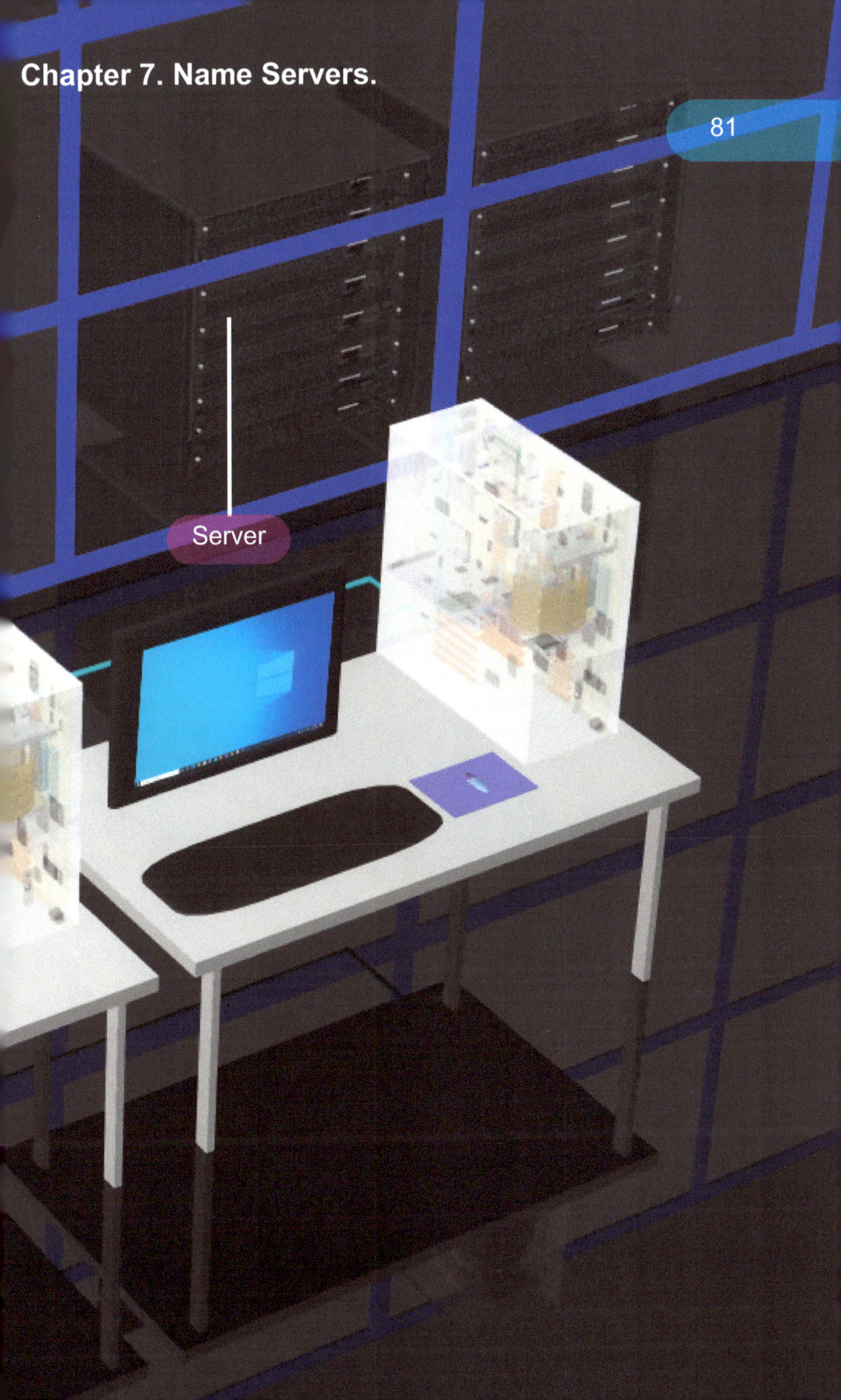
81
Server

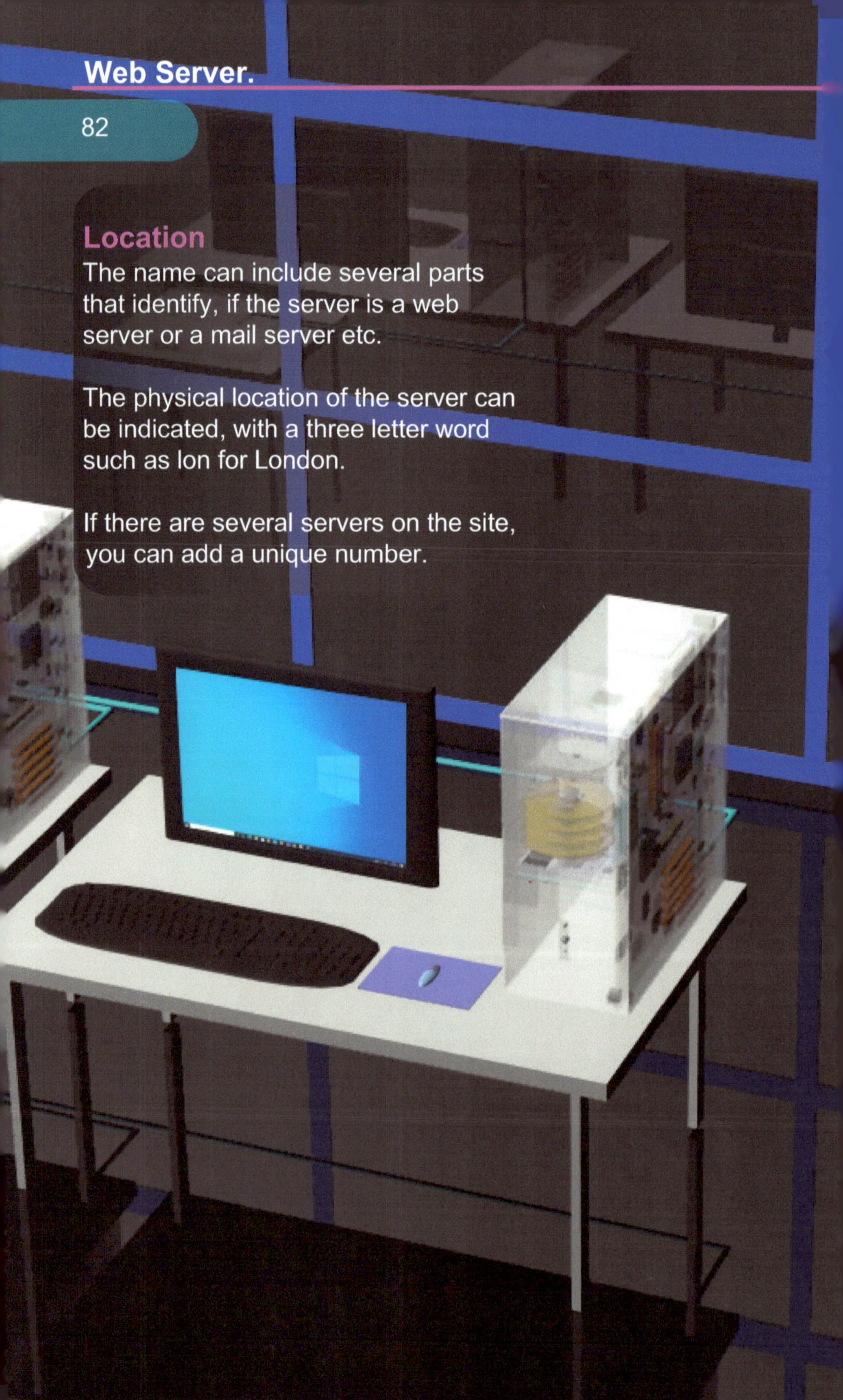

Web Server.

82

Location
The name can include several parts
that identify, if the server is a web
server or a mail server etc.

The physical location of the server can
be indicated, with a three letter word
such as lon for London.

If there are several servers on the site,
you can add a unique number.

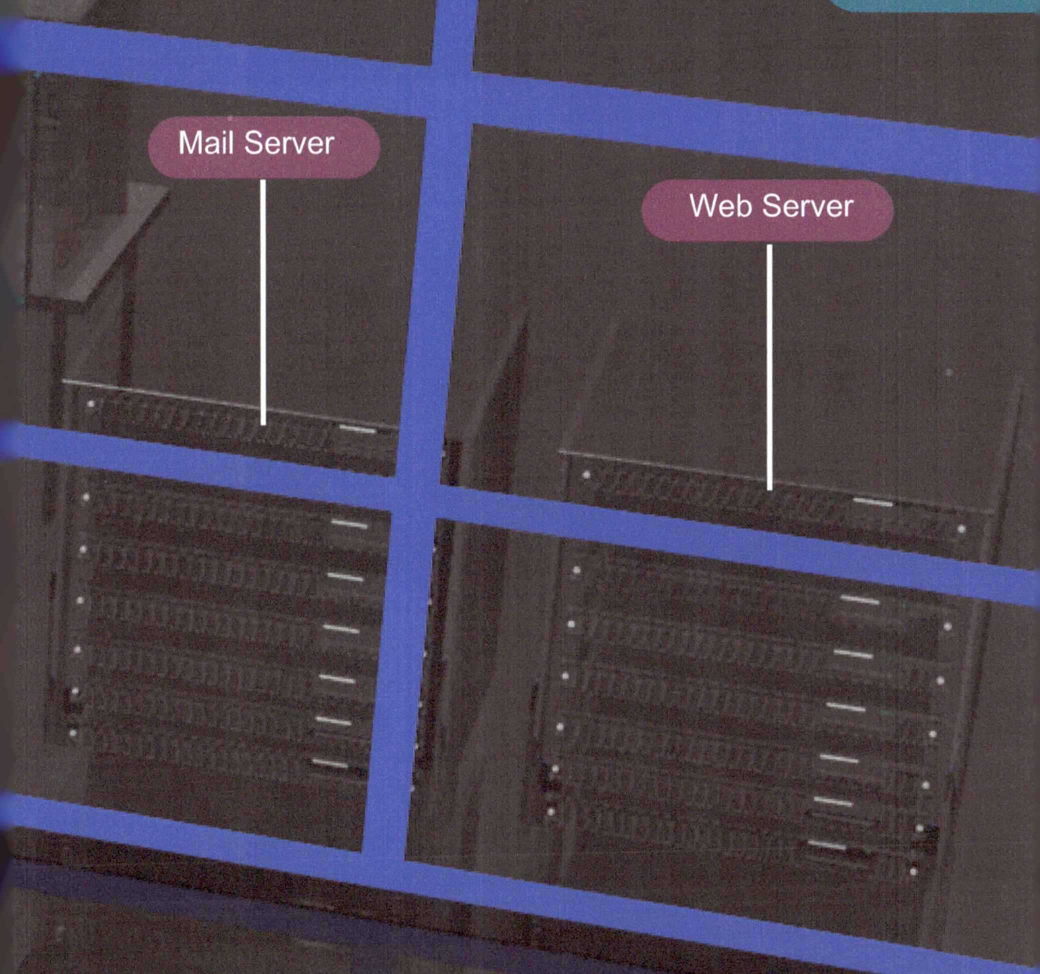

SQL Database

The servers can have different hosting uses.

One server maybe dedicated to hosting a SQL database.

Another server may host web pages.

Other servers may be mail servers to store emails.

For a web server we use three letters:-

www

For the location of the server, in this case London, we use an abbreviation :-

LON

To complete the name we add a unique number :-

Lon-www-001

For a database server the name would be:-

Lon-dbs-010

Lon-www-001
Lon-dbs-010

Chapter 8

Peer to Peer.

P2P

A peer to peer network, allows everyone on that network to access and share files from any computer.

The peer to peer network consists of a network of computers connected together, usually through the internet.

Quite often this type of network is used for file sharing.

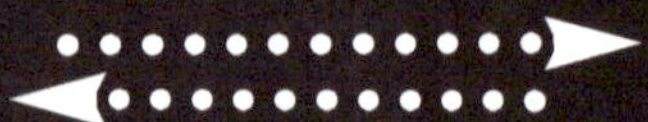

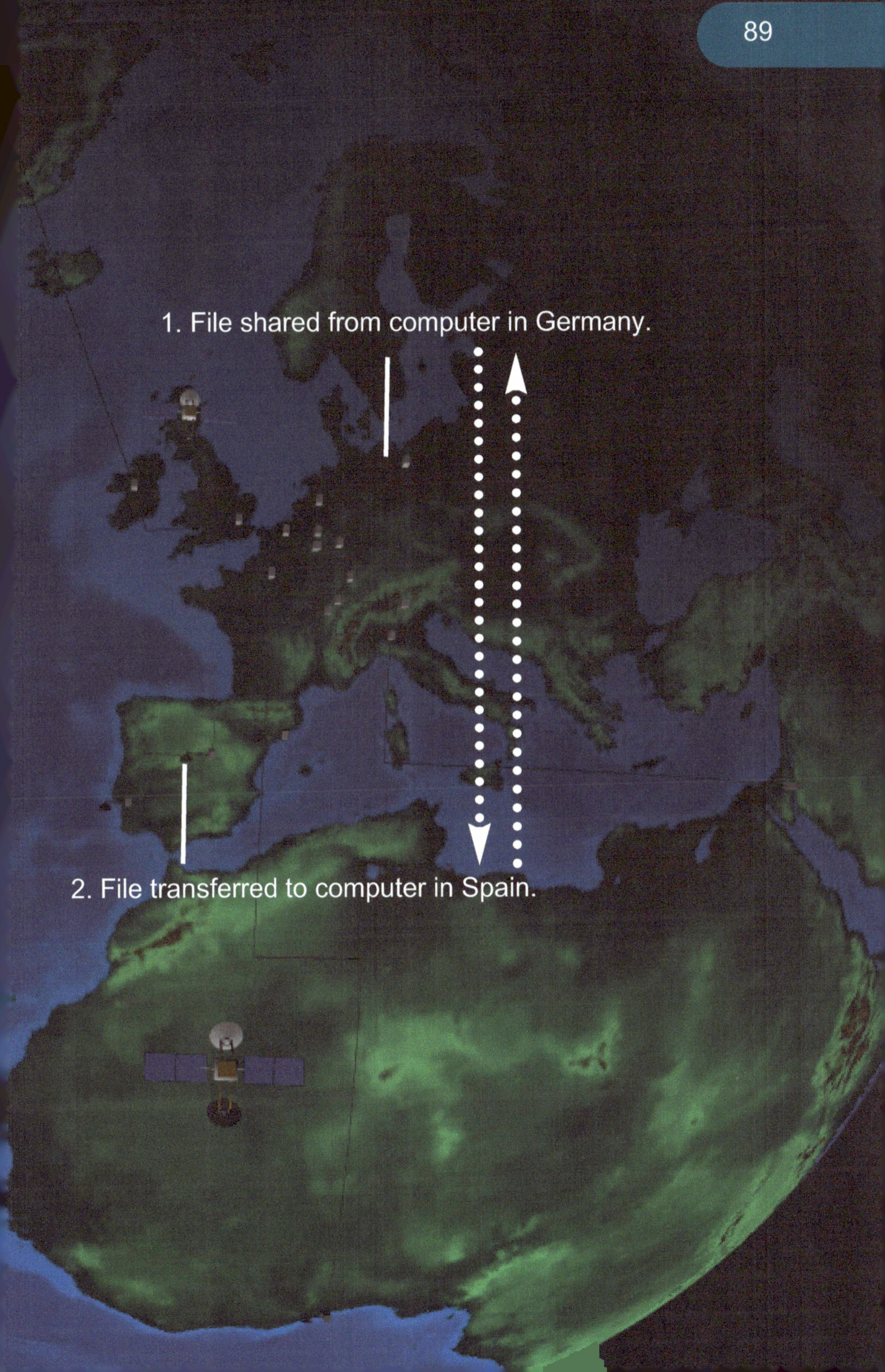

1. File shared from computer in Germany.
2. File transferred to computer in Spain.

File Sharing
In a peer to peer network there isn't as such a single server that files are accessed from, instead each computer acts as a provider of files.

1. Computer with files to share.

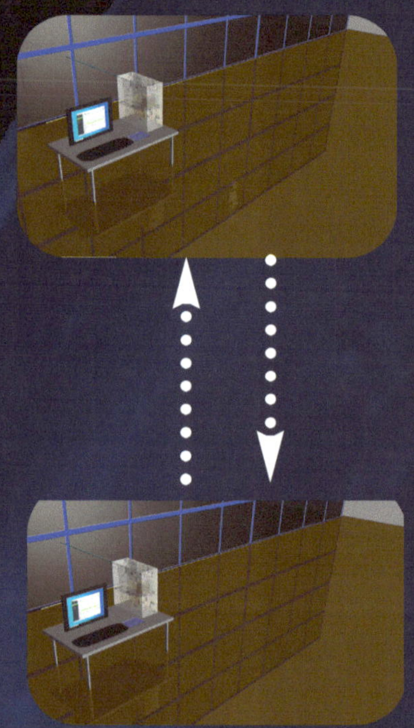

2. Computer requesting files..

Each computer on the internet has the potential to share files.

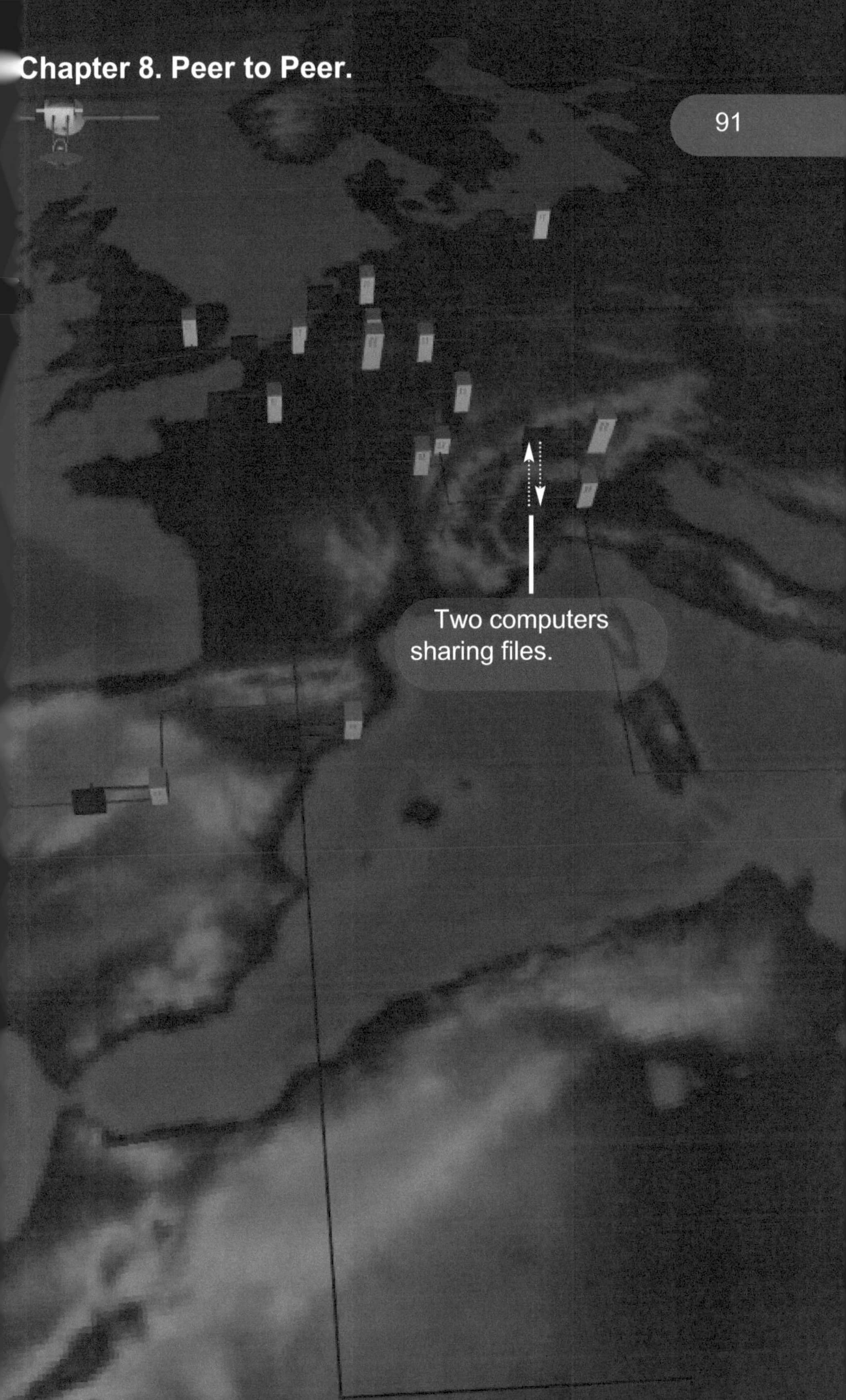
Two computers
sharing files.

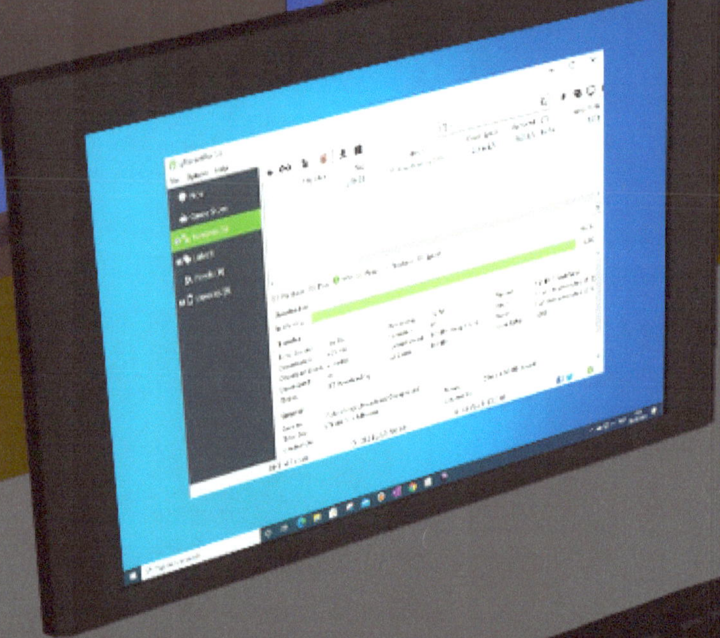

Software

A special piece of software will connect to a directory computer, that lists the files you are publically prepared to share from your computer.

In the directory list will be files that other users are also prepared to share with you.

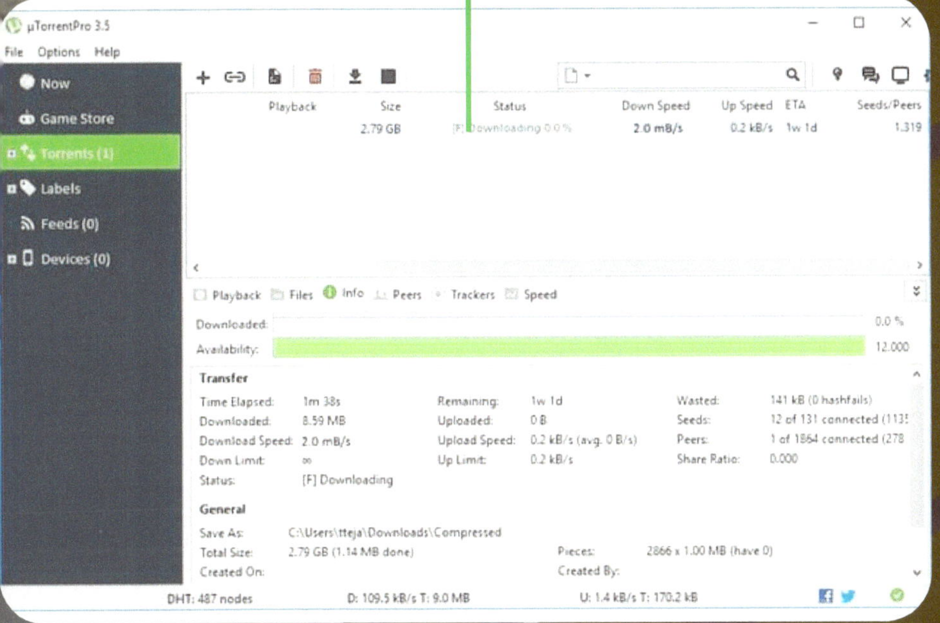

Directory

In the directory list will be files that other users are also prepared to share with you.

P2P Network

You search the directory computer for the file you are looking for, if the file is present on the P2P network.

Download

If the file is available, click on the directory listing and the file will be downloaded.

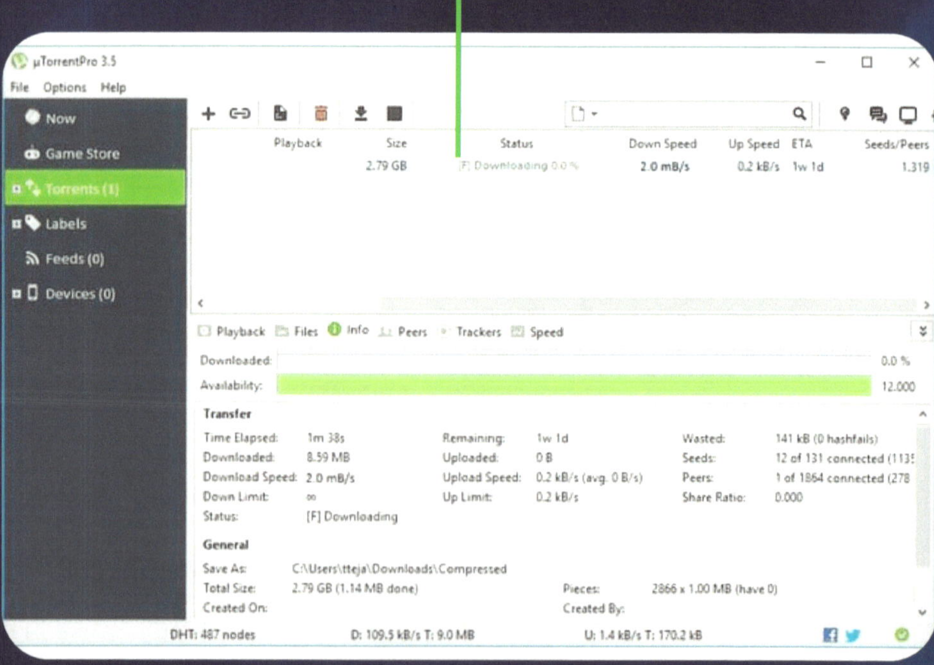

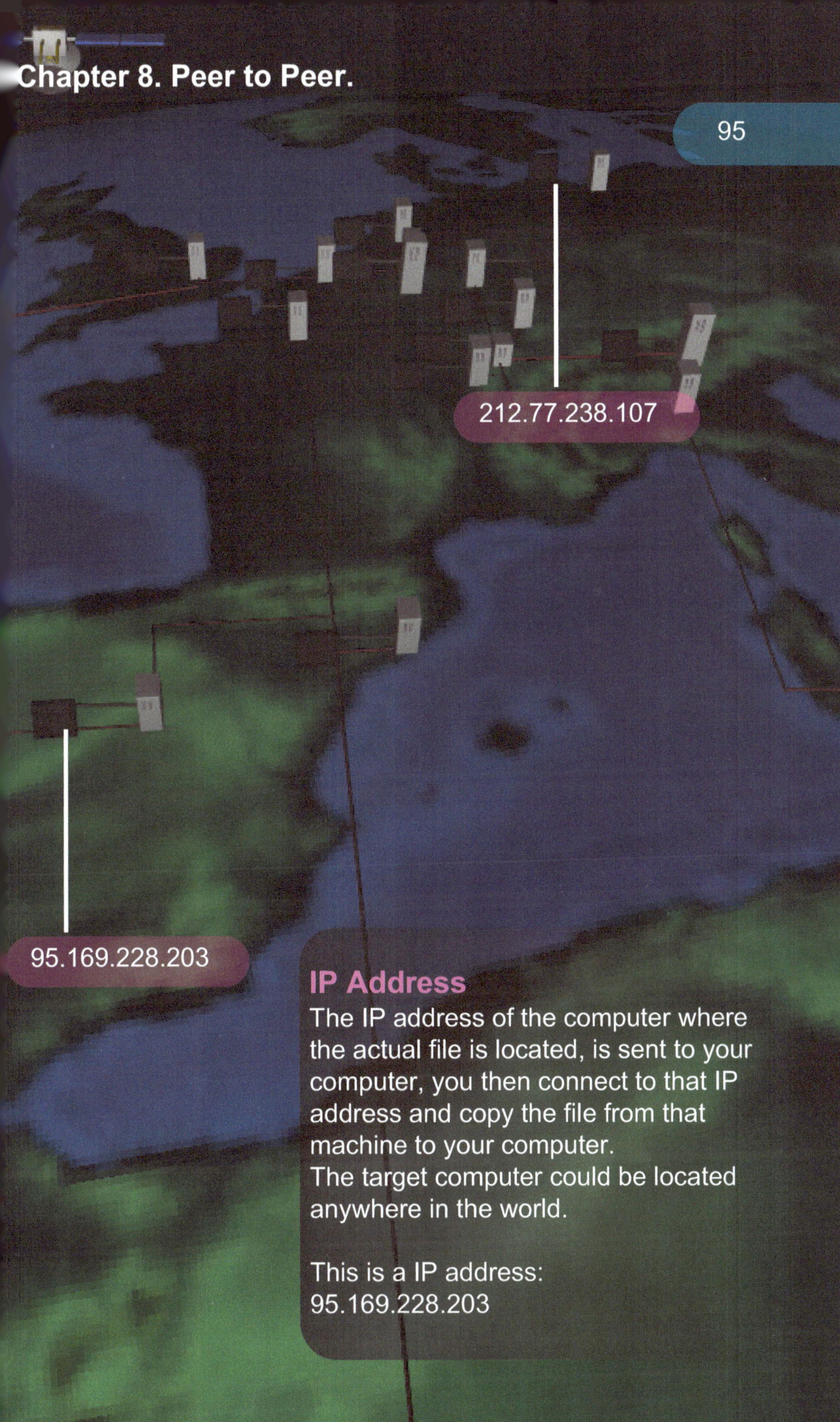

IP Address

The IP address of the computer where the actual file is located, is sent to your computer, you then connect to that IP address and copy the file from that machine to your computer.
The target computer could be located anywhere in the world.

This is a IP address:
95.169.228.203

IP Address

If you have a file that someone wants
on your computer, the directory
server will give them your IP address
and they will download the file from
your computer.
Peer to Peer networks are mainly used
for sharing files across the internet.

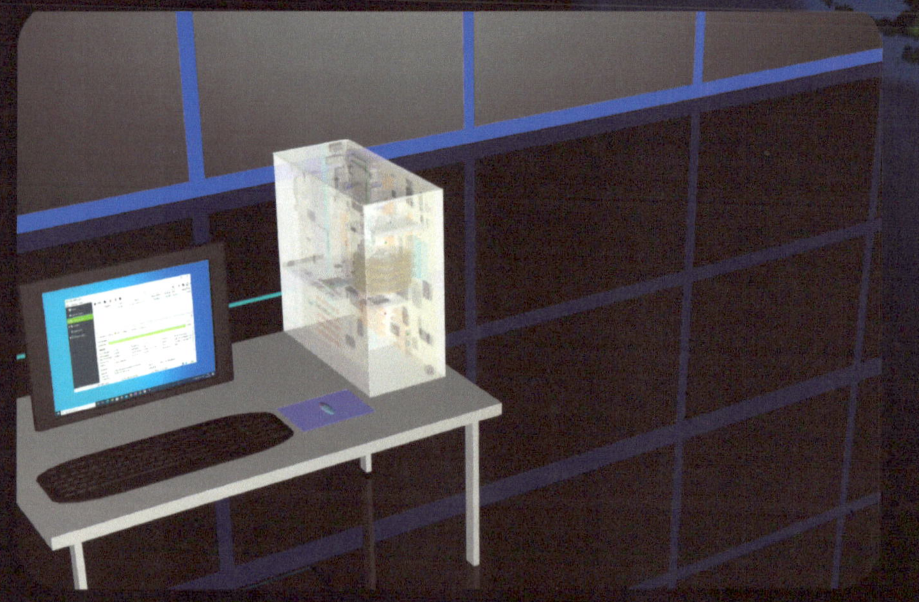

P2P Software

Directory Server

The directory server of the P2P network
you are using, scans the currently
connected computers to see what files
are available.
When you search for a file the server
will return a list of the available files.
In the client software you click on the
listing you wish to download.
The directory server will not have the
file itself, just the IP address of where
the file is stored...